Effective School Leadership in Challenging Times

Education leadership has been subject to a period of turmoil with rapid social change, political demands for excellence, economic pressures for austerity and the influence of technology impacting on leadership roles in multiple ways. This book draws on real examples of practice to identify the key challenges facing educational leadership and how these might be overcome drawing on recent research and interventions that have impacted positively on learner outcomes and teacher retention.

Covering all aspects of leadership including school improvement, vision and values, working with partners and leading change, the book launches the concept of atomic leadership, advocating small steps to change for maximum momentum and large-scale impact. It reveals how leaders can cooperate to trial new ways of learning and disseminate their successes and failures with a new honesty and openness about what works in our schools.

With reflective tasks in every chapter, this text will inspire debate and inform discussion at staff meetings and is essential reading for all school leaders as well as those undertaking master-level courses in educational leadership and or pursuing the National Professional Qualifications in leadership.

Liz Browne has worked in a range of contexts within the field of education, including schools, a further education college, and a university. She is the governor of an OfSTED-rated 'Outstanding' school. As a semi-retired academic she spends her free time delivering training to teachers and academics from across the world.

Effective School Leadership in Challenging Times

A Practice-First, Theory-Informed Approach

Liz Browne

Routledge
Taylor & Francis Group

LONDON AND NEW YORK

First edition published 2021
by Routledge
2 Park Square, Milton Park, Abingdon, Oxon, OX14 4RN

and by Routledge
52 Vanderbilt Avenue, New York, NY 10017

Routledge is an imprint of the Taylor & Francis Group, an informa business

© 2021 Liz Browne

British Library Cataloguing-in-Publication Data
A catalogue record for this book is available from the British Library

Library of Congress Cataloging-in-Publication Data
A catalog record has been requested for this book

ISBN: 978-0-367-18603-6 (hbk)
ISBN: 978-0-367-18604-3 (pbk)
ISBN: 978-0-429-19715-4 (ebk)

Typeset in Optima
by Deanta Global Publishing Services, Chennai, India

This book is dedicated to Zachary, Esme, Leonie and any more grandchildren born to my two sons and their lovely wives. Where the turmoil of an uncertain world has brought challenge and concern, you have brought great joy. And to Roy, who still manages to make me laugh!

Contents

Illustrations

Figures

Tables

# Case studies

Tasks

About the author

Liz Browne started her career in a secondary school in Wiltshire, moving to Somerset where she worked in two secondary schools, one as a head of year, the other as a deputy headteacher. At the birth of her children she took a career break and moved with her husband to Milton Keynes, where she took supply teaching contracts in secondary schools in the area.

Following a move to Oxfordshire, Liz held a number of short-term contracts in schools in Didcot, before securing a job-share position in a local further education college. Once her children were settled at school Liz took a permanent full-time position at Abingdon College as the Head of the Faculty of Health, Social Care and Education. After ten years in the further education sector she secured a post at Oxford Brookes University where she remains today. During her time at the university she has held a number of senior positions including Head of Secondary and Post-compulsory Education, Head of the Centre for Excellence in Teacher Education and more recently Head of the Centre for Educational Consultancy and Development. Liz has two master's degrees, a doctorate and a postgraduate certificate in coaching and mentoring.

Liz has worked closely with the DfE on the workforce reform agenda, has been an associate OfSTED inspector reviewing university-based training provision and has delivered keynote conference presentations across the world. In 2013 she was awarded the title 'Professor of Education'. She now works on a 0.4 contract basis so that she has time to spend with her grandchildren. She believes passionately in the importance of education as a means for social mobility and the tool to give future generations a voice to achieve social justice, peace and world security.

Introduction
Aims and purpose

This book explores the key challenges facing educational leadership in times of uncertainty and change. It draws on recent research and interventions that have impacted on learner outcomes and teacher retention. The book does not shy away from discussing the turbulent times we inhabit whilst exploring what this means for educational leadership. In many chapters the acronym VUCA is applied when discussing pressing issues. VUCA stands for:

- **Volatility:** When change happens rapidly and on a large scale.
- **Uncertainty:** Where the future cannot be predicted with any precision.
- **Complexity:** Where challenges are complicated by many factors and there are few single causes or solutions.
- **Ambiguity:** Where there is little clarity on what events mean and what effect they may have. (Petrie, 2019:7)

Disruption to the world order is creating pressures on school to deliver new and broader learning outcomes to prepare students for uncertain work futures. The pressures are great, but we have to ask where, if not in our schools, can we have a pedagogy of hope and a promise of a stable and bright future?

The UNESCO has articulated clear ambitions for a quality education for all primary aged children by 2030 (UNESCO, 2018). In taking an open view of the challenges ahead a number of leadership approaches are discussed here and offered in support of the challenges we face. It is suggested that, as an overarching approach, leaders, middle leaders and aspiring leaders might take an atomic model for change by trying small steps of innovative practice whilst sampling the tried and tested practices of the past supported by reference to traditional theory. Atomic leadership is proposed as a new way forward, as the clearest solution available and the best approach given the unprecedented times we are experiencing.

Borrowed from the best-selling self-help book by James Clear, entitled *Atomic Habits*, a model is offered to the genre of leadership theory which recommends small-scale change for remarkable results. The aim is to present an honest reflection on the challenges faced in the world of education leadership, to destroy the myth that one theoretical model and approach can solve all problems, and offer solutions based on small interventions that can make a difference. The text draws on real examples from practice to identify the challenges and illustrate how effective leaders are managing change.

School leadership has always been dynamic, but never more so than today. With systems approaches in place leaders can cooperate to trial new ways of learning and disseminate their successes and failures in what will have to be a new honesty and openness about what works in our schools.

The leadership style employed will be more important than ever before. School leaders will need to work collegiately (see Chapter 5) using innovative methods to empower their staff. They will have to be transformative in their approach (see Chapter 6). They will need to be supported and aided by a competent leadership team willing to take responsibility for some difficult issues. Distributed leadership models will have to be applied with effect (see Chapter 4). School leaders will have to support their colleagues and motivate teachers to gain their commitment and loyalty (see Chapter 11).

The global education system has been put to the test. This is creating stresses that can undermine a teacher's self-confidence and self-belief. Chapter 11 addresses the issue of flexible working as a means to retain hardworking staff. Headteachers will have to make decisions based on the effective use of available resources (see Chapter 14) with external pressures coming to the fore that could well 'shake up' the way teaching and learning is delivered in the future. The reliance on technology in times of disaster may become more common, with technological solutions offered to teacher shortages and other restrictions. There will be stresses on the system that cannot be predicted. Environmental and sustainability issues might lead to demands for schools to teach less and be closed for longer periods.

And for our learners, adapting to change will be easier for some families and harder on others particularly where financial hardship or issues of geography limit access to online learning. Equality of experience will be more difficult to achieve with the potential for even greater divisions in society between those that have the opportunity to benefit from education and those who do not. For school leaders this will bring challenges that cannot be planned for or addressed. In such times, taking small steps in an atomic leadership approach might be all that can be done.

School leaders will need to build innovative school cultures that don't rely on past experiences or known practices. The future will always be cast as 'another country' where things will have to be done differently. It will be up to the leaders of the future to protect the things a caring society hold dear, while striving to make things better for all humankind. School leadership was never an easy task, but it is more difficult now than ever before.

 ## References

Clear, J., (2019) *Atomic leadership*. London: Penguin.

Petrie, N. (2019) *Future trends in leadership*. Boston: Harvard University; Centre for Creative Leadership.

UNESCO. (2018) *Accountability in education: meeting our commitments*. Global education monitoring report. UNESCO Publications.

PART I
Leadership as influence

What is educational leadership?

This chapter sets the context for educational leadership in challenging times. It draws on theories past, present and proposed whilst highlighting the volatility, uncertainty, complexity and ambiguity (VUCA) in a fragile world attempting to achieve universal education, peace, harmony and environmental sustainability. This first chapter explores the linguistic association of the words 'leadership' and 'management'. A number of respected academic theories are introduced and a reference grid is provided to illustrate the relevance of leadership theory to all aspects of a range of educational contexts. The concept of 'atomic leadership' is introduced in terms of its relevance for today.

Setting the context

It is clear that educational leadership is experiencing challenging times. It may be that theoretical models, which might support leaders dealing with new challenges, are sadly lacking as new unprecedented times are upon us. In advocating what has been labelled 'atomic leadership' this text supports action, whether small-scale or larger in approach, which is regularly practiced and continued over a period of time. Atomic leadership is based on the mantra that success comes when small efforts, repeated in a systematic way, every day, day in, day out, coupled with the expectation of success and effort can lead to positive change. Based on a model advocated by James Clear, in his book *Atomic Habits* (Clear, 2018), Atomic leadership proposes a model which advocates reducing leadership issues down to the smallest scale possible. The idea is that by impacting on a small, irreducible unit in a larger system in a persistent way, with courage, enthusiasm and determination, change will happen. An atom can produce immense energy and power and so can small interventions in leadership strategy. Small-scale interventions may well be the best way forward given the situations leaders find themselves in today.

The issues faced by leaders trying to chart changing and unknown times can be characterised by the dominance of, in Johansen's words, 'volatility, uncertainty, complexity and ambiguity' (VUCA). In such circumstances a speedy response, proactive engagement and future vision are essential if organisations are to survive (Johansen, 2007).

The term 'VUCA', as used in business planning, is believed to have been first applied in the early 1990s by the American Army College to refer to the multilateral world that appeared after the Cold War and is characterised as:

- **Volatile:** In terms of the type, speed, volume and scale of change.
- **Uncertain:** With our ability to predict the future very much restricted.
- **Complex:** Elements of social media interventions, multiple activities, fear of litigation and confusion and concerns over fake news with no clear connection between cause and effect.
- **Ambiguity:** With a lack of precision and accuracy further hindered by the existence of multiple meanings and interpretations (Raghurampatruni and Kosin, 2017).

These four categories together give voice to the term VUCA to describe a world where change is ever-present, the future is less certain and multiple versions of action are given credible voice with options and choices increasing exponentially in rapid succession (http://www.oxfordleadership.com/leadership-challenges-v-u-c-world/).

In such time of uncertainty, we look to our educational settings to be places of calm and security, and indeed with the turbulence that impacts on the unstable lives of many young people today, schools should be safe places. It is the role of leaders to create, where possible, secure environments where learners and fellow teachers can thrive. At the same time, they have to address some of the turbulence and volatility that impacts on their ability to lead. Leadership of any kind is difficult, but in VUCA times, educational leadership is even more difficult (Dale and James, 2015). Here we examine some of the challenges facing those in leadership roles; we explore a range of appropriate and accepted theories whilst also advocating an atomic leadership style which promotes small-scale action to stimulate change.

Defining terminology

The term 'educational' is applied here to make clear the institutional context for management and leadership. That context could be a school, a college, a university or a virtual learning programme. It might be operating in the UK, or further afield. The area of focus here, then, is a place, in the widest possible perspective, that is legitimate as an educational institution (Bunnell et al., 2016).

In common usage the word 'leadership' is linguistically an abstract noun; that is, a noun denoting an intangible rather than a concrete term, fluid in nature and subject to change as a result of context, time and association. The term 'management' is often used interchangeably with 'leadership', and the resulting ambiguity has led to confusion in the academic literature and in situations where the processes are described. The terms 'leadership' and 'management' are foundational concepts in the description of educational institutions, so clarity of definition and agreed understanding is crucial for theoreticians, writers and those working in educational institutions.

In common usage the words 'leadership' and 'management' may be used interchangeably but in the academic literature the former reflects influence and control, and requires the skills of envisioning, having a major impact, commanding, swaying, cajoling and initiating and introducing new ideas whilst also inspiring others. The term 'leadership' implies the ability to see future needs, to plan and drive change and to direct the organisation's vision. Leadership then is aspirational and directional. Management, in contrast, is operational. Simply described: Leadership is awe-inspiring, management is achieving that vision.

This might be illustrated by reference to the founder of one of the most famous shops in Oxford Street in London, who gave his name to Selfridges. He is famously reported to have said: *'The manager says "go"; the leader says, "let's do this together"'.*

Mr Selfridge saw the need to identify the direction of travel and take others with him to achieve it. His definition implies the ability to inspire others, to have emotional understanding and a personality type which encourages what theorists call 'followership'. It requires a willingness to be involved in what might be described as the 'sharp end' of the core activity. The ability to inspire confidence and motivate others is relevant still today in all organisational settings and none more so than in educational contexts. Today leaders may face issues of organisation size and external pressure which make leadership based on personal contact and knowledge of the individual somewhat difficult to achieve. However, the expansion of social media and technological interconnectivity can help to overcome issues of size; this is explored in the chapter on new technologies.

The term 'management' appears to be disappearing from much of the literature concerning schools. Rooted in the ideas of Weberian ideology the term tends to conjure up connotations of power, with the delegation of tasks and responsibility for the operational running of the educational institution (Bendix, 1977; Lumby, 2017). Managers are often given responsibility to enact the changes required by their leader(s) with managers held responsible if change does not occur (Barker, 2001). The position of manager can be an uncomfortable place to inhabit (Fitzgerald, 2009).

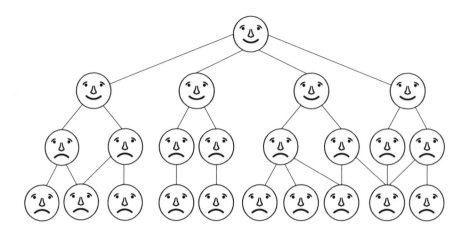

Figure 1.1 Failed leadership portrayed

In schools, colleges and universities, where new challenges occur on a daily basis and external requirements are perpetually in fluctuation, bureaucratic processes are required, but so also is a visionary and adaptable approach which allows for strategic change and the speedy implementation of new initiatives.

In response to criticism of the rigid ideas of bureaucratic theory, UK educational policy has moved away from using the term 'management' and identifies, for example, the National College for School *Leadership*, the requirement for training in School *Leadership* and the appointment of *Leaders* of Education (a term described in Chapter 4). In Finland the idea of teachers as leaders of education is promoted (Sahlberg, 2013). In Canada training for teachers is focused on instructional leadership, i.e. on the professional nature of teaching as the act of leading learning (OECD, 2015).

The decline in the use of the term 'educational management' in the literature and in policy rhetoric could feasibly be hindering the study of educational institutions. Educational institutions employ the terminology in role descriptions and the responsibilities associated with the role of manager constitute an important element of school, college or university operations.

Figure 1.1, drawn by a student of leadership theory, gives voice to some of the problems associated with terminology and offers a stark reminder for leaders who fail to engage with their staff and understand the roles they perform.

The diagram gives a representation of the worst kind of leadership in practice and highlights some of the challenges. To give focus to the term 'effective leadership' and support clarification around the use of the term, seven emerging components of educational leadership are listed as follows:

1. The use of the term 'educational leadership' to describe those in senior positions in an organisational hierarchy has become ubiquitous. International journals

frequently publish articles demanding changes in the art of leadership or in leadership practice. Little research reference is given to management (Lumby, 2017).

2. The term 'leadership' is used to describe the practice of leading (Raelin, 2016). This perspective is central to Cuban's (1988) definition of educational leadership which is 'influence for the achievement of desired goals' (Cuban, 1988,12). Such a view places a premium on interactions that motivate others. These interactions are conditioned by images and instruments which are then put into action (Hawkins and James, 2016; Kooiman, 2001).

3. Leadership can occur in a variety of ways and in a range of settings (Hawkins and James, 2017). It can be direct or indirect and use a range of instruments. It might be carried out, for example, in simple ways, through the written word in a letter to parents, or by being present at weekend school sporting events or meetings.

4. The process of influencing others may be undertaken by any member of the different systems that comprise a whole educational institution (Hawkins and James, 2017). The capacity to influence others is not restricted to those who have 'leader'/'leadership' in their job title. As advocates of distributed leadership argue, for example Harris (2005, 2013), educational leadership is not the sole province of the head of the school/college. Any member of staff may influence others.

5. To seek to understand the nature of educational leadership on the basis of what those in leadership positions do unduly restricts understandings of the complexity of interactions and influence in educational institutions. The act of influence and leadership is interactional (Hawkins and James, 2017), thus leading/influencing others also changes the leader/influencer.

6. Influence in educational institutional contexts may be collective, that is, a group influencing an individual in some way. Dale and James (2015) use the example of scapegoating to illustrate this point, or more positively it might involve a school anti-bullying campaign led by students and teachers alike, leading a change in practice and raising awareness.

7. Finally, because of the importance accorded to leadership and the capacity to influence others, there is a range of theories and models that describe educational leadership, and we turn our attention to these next.

First, though, consider the following exercise which asks, 'Do you have the ability to lead in an educational context?' Answer the following questions with 'Y' for yes, and 'N' for no, and 'NW' for areas where you need to do some work, gain more practise or just become more skilled. Then add up your total (Table 1.1).

Add up your total in each column.

Table 1.1 Leadership requirements

Criteria	Y	N	NW

Communication skills

Can you communicate clearly to a wide range of audiences: Children, parents, fellow teachers, union representative, support staff and administrators?

Can you 'think on your feet' and answer difficult questions with integrity and honesty?

Can you pursue people through logical argument, encouraging them to change their views and support you?

Do you inspire others and make them feel confident in you and in their ability to make a difference?

Interpersonal skills

Do other people trust and respect you?

Can you motivate teams and encourage groups of people to accept your views or strategies?

Are you prepared to intervene when things are not working and tell people directly that they have to change?

Can you be a peacemaker, an honest broker and a fair decision-maker when staff need you to be?

Flexibility

Do you thrive on change and challenge?

Are you prepared to change direction if things are not going as planned?

Are you able to adjust your approach to challenges as the situation or individual requires?

Decision-making

Can you make decisions quickly, always having the information to do so close at hand or at least easily accessible?

Do you make decisions based on evidence and know which sources you can trust?

Are you available and visible if staff need you?

Do you walk around your school and know where difficulties might arise and indeed how to prevent them?

Valuing diversity

Do you encourage respect for individuals and value all staff and pupils equally?

Are you open to ideas for innovation and change from all participants in the organisation: Pupils, teachers, administrators, cleaners, cooks and parents?

Do you welcome others into your school, whilst also observing the requirement to safeguard and protect the pupils in your care?

Success-driven

Are you clear about the strengths and weaknesses of your organisation?

Are you prepared to strive constantly for improvements?

Do you know where and how you and your organisation add value to the life of a young person?

Are you always seeking new ways and new ideas to make your organisation even better?

Problem-solver / innovator

Are you prepared to tackle problems and try out solutions?

(Continued)

Table 1.1 Continued

Criteria	Y	N	NW
Are you good at finding new ways to do things, with a positive outcome?			
Do you make changes to prevent problems before they arise?			
Are you prepared to take responsibility for and publicly acknowledge your problems whilst taking action to prevent future occurrences?			
Results-driven			
Do you always set a good example?			
Do you support your staff and encourage them always to aim to be the best?			
Are you able to inspire and motivate young learners?			
Are you confident in the course of action required to create a continuously improving learning environment?			
Can you communicate your vision for success in a way which motivates others?			
Confidence			
Do you have faith in your abilities?			
Are you able always to remain calm and keep to the decisions you have made?			
Does your public demeanour always inspire confidence?			
Are you prepared to be unpopular in the knowledge that you are doing the right thing?			
Are you aware of your own shortcomings?			

Task 1.1 Self-assessment

So, having completed the exercise above reflect on your personal strengths and weaknesses. Do you have the skills, abilities and confidence to be a good leader? Where do you need to do more work? Has the exercise made you realise that leadership is more complex than you first envisioned? If you are an experienced leader are there any categories missing from the above list? Please record your thoughts and ideas below.

Categorising educational theories and models

There is a plethora of theories that support the student and practitioner working in an educational context (Bush and Glover, 2014; Leithwood and Riehl, 2013). Despite this rich range of theoretical options many students of education and those working in educational context fail to see their relevance. This is explored in more detail in Chapter 2. In an attempt to support the sceptic a summary of theories and models is offered based on the ideas proposed by Connolly et al. (2017) where educational leadership is defined as 'the act of influence within a system which has purpose, requires the influence of order and control, with a range of changing and varied inputs and outputs, has agreed processes and takes place in a specified context requiring responsible actions' (Connolly et al., 2017:15).

For Connolly, then:

Leadership has influence.
Leadership requires purpose.
Leadership needs to be seen in and respond to context.
Leadership involves responsibility.

These four categories create the shape of this book as they are the identifiers for the four parts presented here. In addition, these four categories are adopted to identify a number of well-known and respected leadership theories. The intention behind this tabular approach is to provide an initial guide to readers and researchers when exploring the application of theory to real live situations experienced during the process or study of leadership.

1. Leadership as influence

Leadership theories focus on the purpose of an act of leadership, for example to transform an organisation, whether there be a moral imperative or not.

Chapter 1	Leadership defined
Chapter 2	Atomic leadership
	Collaborative leadership
	Situational leadership
Chapter 3	Visionary leadership
	Transactional leadership
	Transformational leadership
	Learner-centred leadership

2. Leadership with purpose

There is the intention, behind the act of leading, of creating educational institutions that operate within closely organised structures and with a clear vision of how things ought to be.

Chapter 4	Systems leadership
	Distributed leadership
Chapter 5	Authentic leadership
	Atomic leadership
	Data-informed leadership

3. Leadership in context

Leadership has to take account of the situation, to tackle changes and to be adept at adopting new approaches and taking on new challenges. The act of leading is very much changed by the prevailing situation and leaders need to adjust to reflect the challenges put before them whilst always remaining constant to the basic principles which underpin human society.

Chapter 6	Change leadership
	Atomic leadership
Chapter 7	Learner-centred leadership
Chapter 8	Knowledge leadership
Chapter 9	Situational leadership
	Instructional leadership
	Democratic leadership
Chapter 10	Instructional leadership
	Atomic leadership

4. Leadership with responsibility

Leadership is not an isolating act but one that impacts meaningfully on a range of people. Being a leader involves responsible use of resources, the preparedness to work with others and the ability to lead others when the future may seem unclear.

Chapter 11	Collaborative leadership
Chapter 12	Technological leadership
	Leadership for social justice
Chapter 13	Political leadership
	Leadership with integrity
Chapter 14	Preparedness to lead change in challenging times

For readers from the UK the end of every chapter of this text highlights the leadership competences covered in the National Professional Leadership Qualifications for aspiring middle leaders and leaders in English schools. For this chapter, the standard is:

Recognise your own strengths and weaknesses and identify learning linked to your needs.

References

Barker, R.A. (2001) The nature of leadership. *Human Relations*, 54 (4), 469–494.

Bendix, R. (1977) *Max Weber: an intellectual portrait*. Berkeley, CA: University of California Press.

Bunnell, T., Fertig, M. and James, C.R. (2016) What is international about International Schools? An institutional legitimacy perspective. *Oxford Review of Education*, 42 (4), 408–423. doi: 10.1080/03054985.2016.1195735.

Bush, T. and Glover, D. (2014) School leadership models: what do we know? *School Leadership and Management*, 34 (5), 553–571.

Clear, J. (2018) *Atomic habits*. London: Random House.

Connolly, M., James, C. and Fertig, M. (2017) The difference between educational management and educational leadership and the importance of educational responsibility. *Journal of Education Management, Administration and Leadership*, 37 (5), 213–225.

Cuban, L. (1988) *The managerial imperative and the practice of leadership in schools*. New York: State University of New York Press.

Dale, D. and James, C. (2015) The importance of affective containment during unwelcome educational change: the curious incident of the deer hut fire. *Educational Management Administration and Leadership*, 43 (1), 92–106.

Fitzgerald, T. (2009) The tyranny of bureaucracy: continuing challenges of leading and managing from the middle. *Educational Management Administration and Leadership*, 37 (1), 51–65.

Harris, A. (2005) *Crossing boundaries and breaking barriers: distributing leadership in schools*. London: Specialist Schools Trust.

Harris, A. (2013) *Distributed leadership matters: perspectives, practicalities, and potential*. Thousand Oaks, CA: Corwin.

Hawkins, M. and James, C.R. (2016) Understanding leadership in schools: a complex evolving, loosely linking systems (CELLS) perspective. *Presented at the university of the council for educational administration annual convention*, Detroit, MI. 17th–20th November 2016. UCEA: University of Virgina.

Hawkins, M. and James, C. (2017) Developing a perspective on schools as complex, evolving, loosely linking systems. *Educational Management Administration and Leadership*, 4 (56), 235–241. doi: 10.1177/1741143217711192.

Johansen, B. (2007) *Get there early: sensing the future to compete in the present*. San Francisco, CA: Berrett-Koehler.

Kooiman, J. (2001) *Interactive governance*. London: Routledge.

Leithwood, R. and Riehl, M. (2013) What we know about successful school leadership. *Leadership in American Educational Research Association*, 3, 210–219.

Lumby, J. (2017) Distributed leadership and bureaucracy. *Educational Management Administration and Leadership*, 47 (1), 5–19, 2019. doi: 10.1177/1741143217711190.

Office for Educational Cooperation and Development (OECD). (2015) *Out look Canada education policy*. Paris: OECD.

Raelin, J. (2016) Imagine there are no leaders: reframing leadership as collaborative agency. *Leadership*, 12 (2), 131–158.

Raghurampatruni, R. and Kosin, S. (2017) The straits of success in a VUCA world. *Journal of Business and Management*, 5 (2), 16–22.

2 | **What leaders think**

This chapter identifies the challenges faced by educational leaders today. It is based on extensive research which involved conversations with leaders from a range of settings. In placing this chapter in an early part of the text the intention is to illustrate how leadership voice and leadership theory can be joined to offer solutions for practice. The practice of focusing on elements of small atomic changes is advocated for what may appear to be insurmountable problems. Theories of quality leadership and situational leadership are introduced and applied to practice. This chapter highlights that any discussion of leadership and the theories that support the act of leading have to be closely aligned to practice and relevant to the issues faced by leaders today.

For Gunter (2010) we are experiencing a theory practice binary in the field of educational leadership with leaders and students alike facing problems when trying to align leadership theory to the everyday practice of leading education. Most educational leadership theories have been borrowed from the field of business and/or find their roots in the social sciences such as psychology, sociology and philosophy. Such theories, and those generated by educationalists, can offer support to the practitioner when the pressures of change and everyday challenges dispel common sense and cause tension. In an attempt to align leadership theory once more to the practical experience of our current leaders, focus is given to the voice of leaders facing challenges today. Based on their views a range of theoretical perspectives are explored with an aspiration that the theoretical lens might then offer insight to support those facing the leadership challenges of today.

Aimed at focusing leadership at the point of action, rather than theory, research was carried out with 58 leaders of education working across the spectrum of schools, academies, free schools, trust schools and public and private organisations (Browne, 2016). Leaders were interviewed by telephone with the intention of identifying issues they currently face in their role. Data from these interviews were collected and analysed to reveal a number of interconnected themes.

Task 2.1 Your opinion

Before you read the results of the interview you may wish to think about what the issues might be.

The research question posed, after permission was gained to interview the respondent, introductions were given and the nature of our interest set out, was as follows:

'If you had to identify the issues that require your focus the most in your role as a leader of education what would they be?'

The collected data were analysed using a themed approach. The most frequently reoccurring themes are identified here with an explanation provided as to why the leaders expressed concern about these aspects of their role.

The four big issues:

Issue 1: Maintaining quality
Issue 2: Motivating and maintaining high-quality staff
Issue 3: Leading learning
Issue 4: Work/life balance

The issues will be discussed shortly, but first consider the following task.

Task 2.2 Making comparisons

Compare this list of issues with those you identified. How do they differ and why?

Is any difference due to local or regional matters or due to leadership style and approaches? Are there any other reasons for the difference?

Issue 1: Maintaining quality

The first and most often mentioned issue of the four big issues was that of *maintaining quality*. Here leaders talked about the need to set high standards for staff and learners alike. Those interviewed were ever conscious of the data used by OfSTED (the UK audit body) to prompt inspection, maintaining that most of their working week was focused on 'monitoring assessment data, keeping track of attendance, identifying areas of weakness and working with the resources available to introduce interventions that would prevent any slippage in learner achievements' (Primary School Head). For those leaders where the quality scores from OfSTED were not already 'Good' or 'Outstanding', the concern was to achieve this quality kitemark and reduce the likelihood of persistent inspection and monitoring. Even those working in schools designated by the audit body as 'Outstanding' expressed concern at the time spent focusing on staying in a pole position.

It is universally acknowledged that the purpose of inspection and external review, as adopted in schools around the world, is to gauge the quality, rigour and sustainability of schools' internal processes for self-evaluation (McBeath, 2012). This is explored further in Chapter 4 where systems models and theories of distributed leadership are identified as the theoretical model most appropriate for inspiring teachers to work collaboratively to achieve the goals of a self-improving system. Here we focus specifically on the role of the leader in addressing quality issues. The theoretical model proposed in the following focuses on the knowledge leaders need to be effective and establish a high-quality functioning institution.

What does the theory say in relation to quality issues?

The theoretical lens for considering quality issues suggests there are three core components of educational quality leadership. These elements are essential to driving quality improvements in our schools.

They are as follows:

- **Variation knowledge:** An understanding of any variation in performance and the causes of that variation. Leaders working in educational institutions need to understand the weaknesses and strengths of the organisation. Having identified weaknesses, they need to be able to demonstrate appropriate action to correct the issue(s). For example, if a newly appointed teacher is struggling with discipline, the school leadership team should be aware and be able to demonstrate that remedial action and support has been instigated to 1) support the teacher, and 2) ensure pupils receive appropriate teaching to ensure learner success.

- **Knowledge theory:** The understanding of what can be known. An education leader needs a detailed knowledge and understanding of the quality criteria by which the institution will be judged. They need to be confident that their staff are teaching the most recent curriculum and are making appropriate judgements about learner capabilities. The monitoring of learner achievements and confirmation that the school data reflect a fair and accurate picture are essential. Leaders must be aware of the most recent data produced on their institution, predict future patterns and be able to share this with the staff and the governing body. An effective leader will expect questions and challenges pertinent to the school data on pupil attendance and learner achievements. If challenged, an effective leader will be able to accept praise on behalf of the staff and respond well to concerns, by demonstrating that action is already in place to improve the situation.

• **Psychological knowledge:** The understanding of how human beings interact.

Collaborative leadership approaches highlight the importance of staff engagement and commitment to the educational endeavour. Supporting staff and involving them in decision-making is crucial for effective leadership. Schools are diverse communities and collectives embracing staff and students from a range of backgrounds with multiple needs, various political affiliations and cultural beliefs. Leaders need to model respect for difference in all interactions whilst establishing a culture and ethos that protects humanity and aims for constructive engagement.

These three ideas find their roots in what is known as total quality management theory (TQM), a theory which locates knowledge as one of the core elements of good leadership and although first used in marketing to improve customer service, works well when applied to the field of education (Crawford and Shutler, 1999).

Task 2.3 How might quality issues impact leadership?

You may wish to consider how the principles of TQM might impact your approach to leadership, the issues you might need to focus on and the approaches you might adopt.

Issue 2: Motivating and maintaining high-quality staff

The second most reoccurring issue raised by the leaders interviewed related to staff. Given the current shortages of trained teachers in some subjects and geographic regions of the world, this is not surprising. News headlines refer to the challenges of staffing our schools, blaming staff stress, poor morale and limited financial reward. Research carried out by Cambridge University (MacBeath, 2012) to identify why teachers stay in the profession refers to an altruistic commitment and vocational calling. For Hanson (2005) the term 'vocation' involves a personal dimension or 'calling' linked to a social and public facet that impacts on the sense of self, identity and personal fulfilment generated by working with young people. For many educationalists there is a moral and emotional element that pervades their commitment to teaching. Current obsessions with standards of performance and testing (see Chapter 6) add tensions. The leadership challenge is to walk a path which drives improvements whilst also supporting staff for whom the social and emotional welfare of their pupils is the key purpose of their role.

Good leaders understand organisational reliance on well-qualified and committed staff. Taking time to be available, communicating well, sharing important information, offering praise and encouragement and creating opportunities for progression and reward are crucial aspects of a leadership approach aimed at staff retention. Modelling equity and fair practice whilst showing flexibility within the boundaries of reasonableness and being prepared to openly justify policy decisions was identified as a core component for effective leadership.

Teacher shortage is a worldwide phenomenon and problem with the UK experiencing particular problems in recruiting new teachers to the profession. Data from the OECD (2018) (www.oecd.org/education/talis) reports particular shortages in teachers qualified to teach in key subjects worldwide. A further report commissioned by the OECD (2015) titled Preparing teachers and developing school leaders for the 21st century highlighted that one in five school leaders was experiencing a lack of qualified maths or science teachers, a statistic considered inevitably to impact on students' learning. In Turkey, for example, eight out of ten schools experienced staff shortages in key subjects, and over three out of ten in Luxembourg, Germany, Shanghai-China, and the Netherlands.

It is anticipated that by 2030 China will need another 3.5 million teachers, India 3 million and Indonesia 1.2 million. Some countries are making progress with teacher shortages, particularly in Africa. Mozambique claims to have ended its teacher shortage in 2020, while also reducing the pupil-to-teacher ratio. Chad, Guyana and Mali are on track to achieve the same outcome according to current trends (UNESCO, www.unesco_stastical_database_education).

Teacher shortages make the retention of good teachers a vital component of good leadership. Worryingly, the UK data show it to have one of the worst teacher retention rates with only 48%, according to the OECD league tables for longevity in the classroom. Research carried out by NFER revealed that leaving rates are particularly high for early-career teachers in science, maths and languages. This has made finding suitable staff in these subjects increasingly difficult for secondary school leaders and may well create problems for future teacher supply.

How might the theory help leaders experiencing issues with teacher retention?

In the circumstances just described it is important to retain good staff and situational leadership theory offers some useful support. According to situational leadership theory, a leader's effectiveness is contingent on their ability to modify their behaviour to the level of a subordinate's maturity or experience.

The style a leader uses under situational leadership is based upon combining levels of directive and supportive behaviour. Directive behaviour might best be considered as giving an *order* and supportive behaviour as providing *guidance*.

Hersey and Blanchard (1977) focused on four different leadership behaviours based on the levels of directive and supportive behaviour:

1. Telling is where the leader demonstrates high directive behaviour and low supportive behaviour.
2. Selling is where the leader demonstrates high directive behaviour and high supportive behaviour.
3. Participating is where the leader demonstrates low directive behaviour and high supportive behaviour.
4. Delegating is where the leader demonstrates low directive behaviour and low supportive behaviour.

In situational theory the follower's overall maturity, for the purposes of the theory, is a function of two components: i) Their task maturity is their ability to perform the task and ii) their psychological maturity represents their willingness to perform the task. For leaders to retain the staff they want, situational theory, with the guidance it offers on using appropriate leadership styles for participant needs, offers worthwhile advice.

Task 2.4 Reflection

You may wish to reflect on situations when a leader you work with, or indeed you, have used a telling, selling, participative, directive approach. Reflect on the situation and consider whether this was indeed the right approach for the circumstances. Did the approach achieve the desired outcome? With hindsight what might have worked better? Are different approaches required for different people and/or varying circumstances?

Issue 3: Leading learning

Leadership roles were traditionally the only route to promotion for teachers, with most senior leaders, in the past, having experienced a career trajectory from classroom teacher to leader. Since the early days of the UK education system, and indeed elsewhere across the world, the headteacher has wielded a great deal of power (Mortimore, 2013) and today leaders of education may be responsible for a number of schools and have executive powers to manage large school partnerships. There is still the overriding belief that no matter how large the school, or how big the role, the leader of an educational establishment needs to understand education and, at the very least, be a qualified teacher (Mortimore, 2013). This was certainly the view expressed by the leaders interviewed for the research, with issues associated with the confidence and ability to lead learning, one of the regularly quoted concerns. When this was explored in more detail the issue was linked to the size of the school, with the move towards multi-academy trust organisations running multiple schools, the practice of appointing 'leaders of education' and the management of change. Specifically, respondents mentioned the need to keep abreast of curriculum reform, and to effectively monitor student progress whilst implementing effective action and dealing with unavoidable issues, staff absence for example.

What support is available from a review of the theory?

It is generally considered today that leading learning, raising standards and focusing on pupils' achievements are the most important components of a leadership role.
    According to Leithwood and Riehl (2013:2–7) there are five key elements:

1. Leadership has significant effects on student learning, second only to the effects of the curriculum and teachers' instruction.
2. Headteachers and teacher leaders provide most of the leadership in schools, but other potential sources of leadership exist.
3. A core set of leadership practices forms the basics of successful leadership and is valuable in almost all educational contexts. These basics are: Setting directions, developing people, developing the organisation.
4. Successful school leaders respond productively to challenges and opportunities created by the accountability-oriented policy context in which they work.
5. Successful school leaders respond productively to the opportunities and challenges of educating diverse groups of students.

These five criteria emphasise the significant role played by effective leaders with criteria 4 and 5 relating to the personal qualities of the leader themselves. These qualities we explore further in Part II of the text. In this section and in the following chapter more focus rests on the earlier part of the list, to be classified here as 'leadership as influence'.
    The interviews carried out with the 58 educationalists highlighted just how much leaders of education are aware of the need to focus their attention on learning. According to Hallinger and Heck (2001:4) leaders who are focused on learner-centred leadership can influence learning in three specific ways:

1. **Directly:** Where leaders' actions directly influence school outcomes.
2. **Indirectly:** Where leaders affect outcomes indirectly through other variables.
3. **Reciprocally:** When the leader(s) affect(s) the teachers, and vice versa.

Although all three forms of influence can be seen in the work of headteachers and other leaders, it is the indirect effects which are likely to have the greatest influence. This is because leaders work with and through others. Headteachers, deputies, heads of departments and pastoral leaders all rely on colleagues to put into practice agreed ways of working. Whatever leaders wish to see happening is contingent on others putting it into practice. Leaders are reliant on others because their ideas are mediated by teachers and other members of staff. This makes the personal relationship element of leadership a key component. Effective leaders are those who know this and are aware of the indirect effects of their actions (Southwood, 2014).

Effective leaders show awareness of others through three interrelated approaches:

1. Modelling.
2. Monitoring.
3. Dialogue.

In terms of leadership for learning the theory tells us that effective leaders are models for the younger staff in terms of how they approach their role, rigorously monitor learner outcomes and promoting focused conversations (team meetings, staff meetings, meeting with governors). They encourage open dialogue which is student-focused and concerned with helping learners to make the most of their learning experience.

> **Task 2.5 Your organisation**
>
> Consider the approach taken towards learning in your organisation: Do you as a leader emphasise the importance of learning? Is student attainment monitored, are you aware of those learners who require additional help, do you know which areas of the curriculum have been understood and also where additional teaching might be required? Does the organisation encourage learning conversations about pupil progress, value-added measures and whole-class achievement?

Issue 4: Work/life balance (WLB)

The final major area of concern arising from the conversation with education leaders is that of staff wellbeing and work/life balance, including the wellbeing and health of leaders themselves.

All teachers, including headteachers, are entitled to a reasonable work/life balance. This is acknowledged in the School Teachers Pay and Conditions Document (STPCD), which states that:

> Governing Bodies and head teachers, in carrying out their duties, must have regard to the need for the head teacher and teachers at the school to be able to achieve a satisfactory balance between the time required to discharge their professional duties… and the time required to pursue their personal interests outside work. In having regard to this, Governing Bodies and head teachers should ensure that they adhere to the working limits set out in the Working Time Regulations.
>
> (www.stpcd.gov.uk STPCD, Section 2, Part 7, paragraph 53.4, 2016)

As a note of explanation to this statement, governing bodies consist of volunteers from the local community, nominated parent and teacher representatives and the leadership team who work to make strategic decision about the running of the school. Governors work closely with the headteacher to offer challenge and support whilst also playing a role with regard to financial management, including approving pay rises for the headteacher, safeguarding issues and making staff appointments. Their role is generally strategic rather than operational.

In relation to the work of staff, one of the key professional duties of the headteacher is to

> lead and manage the staff with a proper regard for their well-being and legitimate expectations, including the expectation of a healthy balance between work and other commitments.
>
> (www.stpcd.gov.uk STPCD, Section 2, Part 7, paragraph 47.13, 2016)

As a result of the workforce reform initiative it is apparent that some leaders may have taken on more work and this requires careful monitoring (MacBeath, 2012). In this case the school's governing body has a statutory responsibility to support the well-being of the headteacher. In turn, the headteacher has a responsibility to protect their staff from too many evening commitments, long meetings, and poorly timetabled school calendars where, for example, Parents Evening happens during the same week as the school play. Headteachers have a professional duty as set out in Section 2, Part 9, paragraph 57.3 of the 2007 School Teachers' Pay and Conditions Document to 'have regard to the desirability of teachers at the school being able to achieve a satisfactory balance between the time required to discharge their professional duties… and the time required to pursue their personal interests outside work' (www.stpcd.gov.uk, 2016).

Work/life balance involves enabling staff to combine work with their personal commitments and interests. A leader aware of their staff knows that good work/life balance is an essential factor in staff effectiveness and satisfaction, which in turn supports pupil learning. It is in the interest of leadership teams to adopt policies that allow employees to balance their working lives with their personal needs, interests and caring responsibilities. In Chapter 11 a range of examples are offered illustrating good practice around staffing. It is clear to every experienced leader that a lack of work/life balance adversely impacts on all staff. It reduces the chance of good health whilst restricting the individual's ability to balance workload and other activities, such as learning, sport, leisure and family life.

A leadership focused on work/life balance can have positive outcomes, including:

- Reduced stress and sick leave, leading to financial savings on supply cover.
- Improved outcomes for pupils in primary classes in particular where classroom teachers are not affected by ill health absence.
- A more motivated workforce with high morale.
- Better communication within the workplace.
- Making it easier for disabled teachers to stay in the profession when they acquire impairments or when impairments change.
- Improved pupil behaviour and learning as staff wellbeing increases (NUT survey).
- Promoting gender equality, because the long hours associated with full time teaching contracts discourage women seeking promotion and mean women are over-represented in part-time teaching.
- Recognition that working excessive hours might actually reduce staff effectiveness. Staff should be valued for their skills, experience and contribution, not their working pattern.
- Increased job satisfaction.
- Fewer problems with recruitment and retention – a good work/life balance policy will give schools an 'edge' when seeking to attract and retain staff of the highest calibre.
- Work/life balance is not mainly about doing less – it is about maintaining, or even raising, performance by living healthier, more productive, lives.

(Adapted from a NUT publication www.NUT_worklife_balance)

Case study 2.1 Good practice

Since the introduction of assessment without levels (see Chapter 6) class teachers are required to record and monitor individual learner progress against the key performance indicators newly introduced in the new national curriculum. Aware of the additional pressure that this has put on staff, one headteacher in an average size primary school now takes a 30-minute assembly once a week, without the expectation of staff attendance, so that the teachers can spend time on record-keeping. The leadership team has designed its own record-keeping tool mapped against the performance indicators which is updated electronically thus simplifying the process and reducing the time teachers need to take to update their records.

What does the theory tell us about work/life balance?

There are a range of models and theories that have been proposed to support under-standing of the positive and negative pressures that work can exert on the human psy-che. Calls for work/life balance (WLB) have to be viewed in the context of increased demands on teacher performance, reduced funding, teacher performance reviews, heightened parental expectations, student achievement ambitions and publicly avail-able school outcome data. These issues, and many more, place additional pressures on leaders and teachers with employment contracts now requiring that organisations and school leaders effectively manage their employees' wellbeing, stress and job sat-isfaction (Greenhouse and Powell, 2006). Research has identified a clear connection between the way people are led and the smooth running of an organisation (Purcell, 2002:1). In other words, the issue of WLB is inextricably linked to teacher retention and, ipso facto, student achievement.

Work/life balance has been defined as 'satisfaction and good functioning at work and at home with a minimum of role conflict' (Hyman and Summers, 2004:751). As such, it is sometimes characterised by 'the absence of unacceptable levels of conflict between work and non-work demands' (Mellor et al., 2001:179). Thus, when demands from the work and non-work domains are mutually incompatible, conflict may occur. For this reason, a lack of balance between work and non-work is commonly concep-tualised as work/family conflict or work/non-work conflict (Spinks, 2004; Walters and Bardoel, 2006). Such conflict can occur both when work roles interfere with non-work roles and vice versa. This is generally known as 'the conflict model' and is the one most used to describe situations where tensions and pressures exist if staff and leaders are experiencing too much pressure in one aspect of their lives.

For some staff a working life might compensate for something that is lacking in their family life, perhaps children, companionship or general satisfaction. In such cases work can become all-consuming and work-related issues may dominate the whole life of the individual. It is important that such staff and also leaders are helped, where possible, to achieve a balance in their lives, although the right of the individual to privacy should always be paramount. Where individuals are willing to share infor-mation about their private circumstances the business of leadership becomes a little easier. Individuals who exhibit all-consuming approaches to work are said to operate within the 'compensation model,' where what is lacking in one area (i.e. demand, satisfaction) is compensated for by the other.

Another view of WLB described as the 'instrumental model' identifies how activ-ities in one area might work to facilitate success in the other. So, a leader, for example, who is good at sport, may be able to use that skill to motivate disenchanted learners and staff. Having additional skills and abilities can help teachers and leaders gain the respect of their colleagues who begin to see them as people outside a formal context, worthy of recognition.

The 'enrichment perspective' argues that some people are capable of involvement in multiple roles with the benefits of improved attention and energy to mitigate the stress associated with their position. This view is similar to the 'expansionist theory' which claims that performance in each role is enhanced by the involvement in other roles.

What does this mean for leaders?

Leaders have a statutory role to ensure that their colleagues can benefit from reasonable demands on their time with freedom for the pursuit of other interests outside the workplace. It is helpful perhaps in some circumstances for a leader to know what motivates their staff, to know which ones require help with balancing work and the 'other side of their lives' and also to know who works well under pressure. Obviously, leaders in large organisations cannot be aware of every member of staff and need to rely on information from others, or delegate this task to other responsible leaders in the leadership team. The point here is one of 'knowing' and 'understanding' people when taking on a leadership role. When promoting colleagues or asking individuals to take on additional roles it is important for leaders to think about the impact this request might have on the individual concerned. And, for leaders themselves, care needs to be taken to ensure that they safeguard their time and don't take on too much responsibility. In future chapters the leadership theories discussing distributed leadership allow this point to be explored in more detail.

Conclusion

Interviews were carried out with 58 leaders of education with the aim of understanding better the issues faced by leaders operating in our schools and colleges today. Four key themes or interlinking issues were identified. These themes of maintaining quality, motivating and maintaining high-quality staff, leading learning and work/life balance have been discussed and the theory associated with each theme examined here is an attempt to offer some answers to the issue faced by educationalists operating today.

The standards for the National Professional Qualification for School Leaders explored in this chapter include:

> Use a range of techniques to gather evidence on teaching quality and the impact of interventions across a school.
>
> Anticipate other peoples' views or feelings and moderate your approach using personal reflection and awareness.

References

Browne, E. (2016) Leadership conversations – unpublished research carried out on behalf of the Institute for Learning.

Crawford, L. and Shutler, P. (1999) Total quality management in education: problems and issues for the classroom teacher. *International Journal of Educational Management*, 13 (2), 67–73. doi: 10.1108/09513549910261122.

Greenhaus, J. and Powel, K. (2006) The intersection of work-family roles: individual, interpersonal, and organisational issues. *Journal of Social Behavior and Personality*, 3, 23–44.

Gunter, H. (2010) A sociological approach to educational leadership. *British Journal of Sociology of Education*, 31 (4), 519–527.

Hallinger, J. and Heck, P. (2011) Conceptual and methodological issues in studying school leadership effects as a reciprocal process. *School Effectiveness and School Improvement: An International Journal of Research, Policy and Practice*, 22 (2), 41–52.

Hanson, J. (2005) Teaching and the sense of vocation. *Educational Theory*, 44 (3), 259–275.

Hersey, P. and Blanchard, K.H. (1977) *Management of organizational behaviour*, 3rd ed. *Utilizing human resources*. New York: Prentice Hall.

Hyman, J. and Summers, J. (2004) Lacking balance? Work-life employment practices in the modern economy. *Personnel Review*, 33(4), 418–429.

Leithwood, K. and Riehl, C. (2013) *What we know about successful school leadership*. New York: American Educational Research Association.

MacBeath, J. (2012) *Keeping abreast of policy changes at the local, national and international level*. Cambridge: Cambridge University Press.

Mellor, S., Mathieu, J.E., Barnes-Farrell, J.L. and Rogelberg, S.G. (2001) Employees' non-work obligations and organisational commitments: a new way to look at the relationships. *Human Resource Management*, 40 (2), 171–184.

Mortimore, P. (2013) *Education under siege*. Bristol: Policy Press.

Purcell, J. (2002) Introduction to. *Human Resource Management Journal*, 12 (2), 234–242.

Southwood, G. (2014) *Educational leadership | Learn how to inspire staff.* www.irisco nnect.com/downloads/school-leaders (accessed 19.5.18).

Spinks, N. (2004) Work-life balance: achievable goal or pipe-dream? *The Journal for Quality and Participation*, 27 (3), 4–11.

Walters, M. and Bardoel, E. (2006) Work-family policies in the context of higher education: useful or symbolic? *Asia Pacific Journal of Human Resources*, 44 (1), 67–82.

www.oecd.org/education/talis. OECD data on teachers from across the world add 2018 data when available.

www.NUT_worklife_balance. Section 2, Part 9, paragraph 57.3 of the 2007 school teachers' pay and conditions document (accessed 15.5.2019).

www.unesco_stastical_database_education_2018 (accessed 12.5.19).

www.stpcd.gov.uk. STPCD, Section 2, Part 7, paragraph 47.13, 2016.

3 The place of vision, mission and culture in a changing world

The culture of a school, college or university is said to be created through the articulation of a mission or vision and through clear expression and enactment of core values. This chapter explores how mission, vision and values influence educational leadership whilst exploring the importance of an institutional culture that promotes effective learning and organisational coherence.

Any discussion of mission, values and culture in the context of leadership needs to take into account the perceived universal importance of education and its function and purpose. This chapter records the views of social scientists who research education ideology worldwide. Taking a chronological approach, it investigates the development of the concepts of vision, mission, values and culture, with changes in language identified over time. International approaches are explored based on ideas generated in China, Australia and the UK. In aligning the ideas of this chapter to leadership theories, the role of visionary leadership is explored, with reference made also to transactional leadership, transformative and learner-centred leadership.

First, some history

A quality educational experience has been the privilege of the rich across the world for hundreds of years. Schools established to educate those with the funds to pay, tended, in the UK, to have religious benefactors such that the motto for such schools may still contain reference to this fact. For example, Abingdon School, a boy's independent school founded in 1256, has the motto:

Faith and industry

Leys School in Cambridge, founded in 1875 and attended by James Hillier, who wrote the novelette 'Goodbye Mr Chips', a film worth watching to see a variety of leadership approaches in practice, has the motto:

In faith, trust.

The Society for the Propagation of Christian Knowledge (now known as SPCK), established in London in 1699, reached across to the Americas, the Indian nations and the Caribbean Islands, carrying out missionary work designed to provide education for the poor across the world. Promoted by concern over the growth in vice and immorality, school mottos articulate Christian values of honesty and faith, for example. St George's School in Chennai, India, founded in 1715, had and still has to this day, the motto:

Trust in God and do the right.

During the industrial revolution the function and purpose of schools shifted away from ideas about humanising and socialising the poor and depraved to those associated with the production of a labour force required to build for the future. When the landed gentry needed the poor to work in the fields education for civilisation and social coherence was important: When industries developed the populace needed to be skilled, with acceptable levels of literacy, numeracy and technical knowledge. As the industrial revolution expanded across the world so did the need for schools. This was accompanied by the expectation of universal education which incidentally in 2014 was still only available for 71% of children under the age of 12 in parts of sub-Saharan Africa (UNESCO 2015).

For social scientists such as Durkheim (translated here in 2007) and Parsons (translated here in 1991) education has three key roles:

1. **Passing on society's culture** – education functions as a key mechanism through which a new generation of children acquire the 'central' norms, values and culture of their society. This unites or glues people together by giving them shared values, what sociologists term a value consensus, through the hidden curriculum.
2. **Socialisation** – Durkheim argued that schools are a 'society in miniature' – a small scale version of the wider society in which people live and work. Schools take over the primary socialisation role of parents. This means schools are sites of secondary socialisation. They provide a bridge between the 'particularistic'

values of the family and the 'universalistic' values of contemporary industrial society.

3. **Providing a trained and qualified labour force** – schooling provides society with people equipped with the right skills to work in the jobs required for society to thrive and be economically secure.

Given how ideas about education have changed over time school mission statements and declared statements of core values have also changed to reflect societal change. A review of statements today will show a decline in religious language, unless the school has a specified religious affiliation, and an increased focus on achievement, excellent, equality issues and safeguarding.

Given the divergent population living in some jurisdictions, school mission statements might feasibly reinforce the culture norms of the region. Some mission statements in the UK, for example, reflect the government call for British values:

> to create and enforce a clear and rigorous expectation to promote the fundamental British values of democracy, the rule of law, individual liberty and mutual respect and tolerance of those with different faiths and beliefs. (DfE, 2014)

Comparing the Chinese and British perspectives

The language used to express school culture and values in the Chinese system tends to be phrased in a different tone than that used in Western economies. The use of voice in the Chinese system is active, it is bold, precise and succinct. This was demonstrated in a small-scale research project carried out with 40 school leaders from China (Browne, 2019). The research revealed a common theme of 'integrity' as the key word in the statements of 63% of those interviewed. All statements were in an instructional tone for pupils to follow and included some of the following:

> Integrity and perseverance.

The call to:

> Aim high.

as found in 20% of responses.

Xiamen Wuyuan Experiment School calls students to:

> Love your country
> Love your school
> Be a useful person, giving to society.

The language used in UK schools tends to be more discursive than that used in China and indeed the process by which the statements are determined may, realistically today, be a negotiated one as in case study 3.1.

The collective act of creating a vision for a school can be a leadership 'tactic' as in the following when a new head was appointed to change the turn around a specific school. The leadership approach here would be characterised as leadership with influence (see Chapter 1) and categorised as visionary leadership, with a confident headteacher clearly setting out what they want for the school. To achieve this vision, they adopt a number of strategies and leadership styles starting with a transactional approach, moving to a transformative and then to a learner-centred approach. The case study illustrates that different approaches are required in different circumstances, as various challenges materialise.

Transactional: This approach to leadership requires the negotiation of tasks as part of a clear strategy. It is a highly focused approach, often adopted to create a 'quick fix', focused often on improving standards and not likely to be adapted until the end goal has been achieved (Smith and Bell, 2015). It is best achieved when leaders argue that something is essential in the short term to achieve a desired aim. This was the approach adopted by world leaders during the COVID-19 pandemic when countries enforced a stay-at-home policy with the promise that 'things will return to normal, you will see your loved ones again'.

Transformative: Northouse (2004) described transformational leadership as 'a process that changes and transforms individuals'. Concerned with emotions, values, ethics, standards and long-term goals, it requires the leader to establish relationships with their staff to support their aims, where appropriate, whilst respecting the staff as human beings. Furthermore, as Bass (1985) advocated, by engaging in transformational leadership behaviours leaders transform their followers who change from being 'self-centred individuals to becoming committed members of a group, able then to perform at levels far beyond what normally might have been expected' (Antonakis et al., 2004:175).

Learner-centred: This involves leaders working to establish professional communities to meet the objectives of the school. Here leaders become more involved in learning, even if indirectly, with student outcomes affected in a positive way because leaders create the effective conditions for learning to take place (Stoll, 2019; Southworth, 2011).

The following case study is interesting in the articulation of a clear plan and intention when a new head took over a school which was by all sense and purposes experiencing some difficulties.

Case study 3.1 Fitzharrys School

When appointed as the head of a school which became rated as 'inadequate', but which now receives positive reports from the UK school's inspectorate (OfSTED), the newly appointed head knew things had to change. Right at the start of his tenure Jonathan involved the whole school community in a redesign of the school motto and values statement. And, if you talk to Jonathan, the headteacher of Fitzharrys School, Abingdon, Oxfordshire, the conversation is about 'our school', 'our community'. From his first engagement with the school Jonathan's ambition was to create a nurturing environment, to model respect for each person in all interactions and to lead with moral purpose.

Change was not implemented quickly, nor did it come imposed directly from the leadership team. The redesign of school values, vision and mission was an iterative process, with Jonathan spending the first six months modelling the behaviours he wanted the school to adopt, followed by a celebration of what was achieved and a reaffirming of the ethos the school now represents.

From the start of his headship Jonathan focused on the school motto, its values and mission. At his first school assembly in front of staff and students, and again at a parents meeting, Jonathan talked about the acronym TEAM – Together Everyone Achieves More. He then put in place a number of meetings with teachers, pupils and parents and together they created a new vision statement for the school. The outcome is interesting in a number of specific ways:

1. The positive message of hope, the use of the words 'optimism and pride' alongside 'the capacity for curiosity, courage and independence'.
2. The promise of a better future not just for the pupils but staff as well.

The statement has a collaborative tone whilst also offering high aspirations for those who learn and work there. The school vision is presented in Table 3.1.

Table 3.1 Fitzharrys School vision

Fitzharrys' ethos is underpinned by our key values of **G**rowth, **O**wnership, **A**chievement, **L**eadership and **S**uccess (GOALS).

Students and staff at Fitzharrys are active, enthusiastic and engaged. As a school, we are up for any challenge, buoyed up by the optimism and pride that comes from being part of something special.

Success at Fitzharrys is founded upon high quality teaching and learning. We cultivate curiosity, courage and independence, fuelling a passion for learning in all students and staff to shape confident, creative, resourceful and resilient individuals. This culture builds character, creating a springboard for further success as everyone progresses in their education, career and life.

How did the school arrive at this mission statement?

In the words of Jonathan, the headteacher:

> This is not 'my' school; it is our school. This is and was a joint endeavour. You need to begin with the end in mind, considering what type of school and community do you want to create. How will the ethos be evident as you walk around and speak to children? Why will colleagues display dogged determination to keep improving, what compelling reason will they have? The vision for the school must be powerful, clear and well-communicated. The moral purpose behind what you do needs to be understood by everyone; pupils, parents, support staff, teachers and governors, and it must underpin all that you do. It is too easy to be swamped by tasks, meetings, problems. Establish your 'end', communicate the vision and then unfailingly base everything you do on achieving that.
>
> (Interview with headteacher of Fitzharrys School, 12.5.19)

Jonathan's ambition was to create a caring environment, the type of environment he describes as usually found in effective primary schools, with care and compassion at the centre along with stretch and challenge. The approach follows that advocated by Dr Raphael Wilkins when he was President of the UK College of Teachers. For him, school leadership upholds values, and engages critically with imposed ideas and the politics of knowledge to transition spaces of negotiation (Wilkins, 2017:3).

Visionary leadership

The approach adopted in this case study mirrors the definitions offered by Bush and colleagues of visionary leadership, or 'developing, articulating and implementing' a shared vision of learning' (Bush, 2007:23), with the school success data offering empirical evidence of how promotion of a caring environment can change a school and create learners who feel valued, happy and willing to engage.

What is a visionary leadership style?

Visionary leaders are those who hold a good understanding of the 'bigger picture' and are able to communicate using their relevant experience confidently. A real visionary leader will not only explain where people are going, they will also be able to explain why getting there is important. What is really impressive about how visionary leaders achieve this is the way in which they enthuse people and motivate them. Visionary approaches are best employed when:

- A new direction is needed.
- If a team or group is in need of clear direction.
- Time is taken to understand what motivates the team.
- An explanation is offered as to why change is need.
- Leaders can clearly justify the benefits of change.
- Support is available for teams in the change process, with shortfalls recognised and support available where needed.

A visionary leadership style is celebrated as having a positive effect on school environments and staff when it involves team discussion and negotiation. Staff in educational institutions have traditionally looked to school leaders for direction but also for a chance to themselves be involved in decision-making. A leadership style which confidently presents a vision and then sets aside time and space to negotiate the detail of that vision and gain commitment to it is incredibly effective in a range of circumstances, not least in times of change, when new policy initiatives impact on practice or where staff appear demotivated and disillusioned.

In case study 3.1, visionary leadership was required to turn around a school experiencing challenges. The headteacher had to be confident in where he wanted to take the school and clear in how he wanted to get there. But this is not the only leadership style that he adopted. He knew that some teams were dysfunctional, that he needed to resolve tension and conflict. With groups of staff, in specific subject areas, he adopted a more affiliative, collaborative leadership style. Working with specific teams within the organisation involved working at a micro level, talking to individuals, trying to see their point of view and understanding longstanding differences. Collaborative leadership approaches are often required when drastic changes are required. In Jonathan's words: 'It is no good holding a vision if you don't work with your staff teams to create it and you don't motivate your staff to work with you'.

Transformational and collaborative leadership theories focus on the effective elements of leadership. Northouse (2004) described transformational leadership as 'a process that changes and transforms individuals. It is concerned with emotions, values, ethics, standards, and long-term goals, and includes assessing followers' motives, satisfying their needs, and treating them as full human beings' (2004:169). Further, as Bass (1985) advocated, by engaging in transformational leadership behaviours a leader transforms their followers. In reality this means that when 'followers are changed from being self-centred individuals to being committed members of a group, they are then able to perform at levels far beyond what normally might have been expected' (Antonakis et al., 2004:175).

Vision statements from organisations working with the younger age range often focus on themes of nurture, support and aspiration. The following statement places high importance on inclusion creating a welcoming and all-encompassing message.

> At Roseberry Primary & Nursery, we provide a high-quality inclusive education in a safe and nurturing environment, to inspire our pupils to foster a love for learning which enables them to achieve their full potential and equipping them with the skills to adapt in our ever-changing world.

In addition, it promises to instil a love of learning in children and to allow them to develop their full potential and cope with the challenges faced in society today.

The vision of the second school with a religious affiliation offers a clear statement of commitment to the values of the Catholic faith. It reads:

> The mission of Cardinal Hume School is to develop each member of the school community so that everyone involved can reach her/his potential in the light of the teaching of Christ and the values portrayed by the Gospels.

There is still an expectation in UK schools that any headteacher applying to lead such a school would be an active member of the Catholic Church.

Mission and vision: Are they different?

The terms 'mission' and 'vision' might be used interchangeably and whilst there might be some confusion in application there appears to be general agreement in the education community on the major distinctions between them. A vision statement expresses a hoped-for future reality, while a mission statement declares the practical commitments and actions that a school believes are needed to achieve its vision.

So, for example the mission statement for Ivanhoe School in Southern Australia is:

Mission Statement

Ivanhoe Primary School provides a positive, vibrant and inspiring environment where students are valued and encouraged to succeed in becoming life-long learners.

And the vision or aspirations for the future are:

Vision Statement

Ivanhoe Primary School encourages the development of the whole student. Our aim is to support learners in becoming curious, reflective and critical in their thinking as global citizens.

By inculcating the values of:

Values

Confidence, Independence, Persistence, Resilience, Respect.

It is recognised in practice and in the academic literature that compelling, well-articulated mission and vision statements can:

- Help a school community reflect on its core educational values, operational objectives, purpose as a learning institution and hoped-for results for students. By asking tough questions about what the school was founded to achieve, and by looking at where it is in relation to where it wants to be, a school can become better organised to achieve its goals and more focused on the practical steps needed to achieve them.

- Function to rally support for core educational values or an improvement plan, or to mobilise the staff and community to move in a new direction or pursue more ambitious goals. By creating a 'shared mission' or 'shared vision' – that is, developing the public commitments with the involvement of teachers, staff, students, parents and community members – a school can be honest about the challenges it faces and clarify what it hopes to accomplish, why it matters and what may need to change.
- Focus the school's academic ambitions. In some institutions, teachers and lectures work in isolation; also some academic departments may adopt their own approaches to key activities.

    Mission and vision statements can help educators make decisions that are 'aligned' with the vision and mission leading to a coherent and efficiently, purposefully and effectively run organisation.

Task 3.1 Review of mission and vision

Review the mission and vision statement for your organisation. Is it a statement of intention, does it clearly set out what is to be achieved, is it recognised by your colleagues? An interesting research project might involve reviewing the language of the statement(s) and asking colleagues for their views on its relevance for the situations we face today.

Many researchers maintain that successful schools are built around a clear sense of vision and purpose. Leithwood and Riehl (2013) identify the building of a vision and setting direction as the common element of effective leadership qualities comprising the repertoire of all successful leaders. Day (2010) cites setting values and vision as the first of eight key dimensions of successful school leadership; and Barber et al. (2010) argue that setting the vision for a school is one of the biggest contributors to success across schools globally. In schools facing challenging circumstances it has been found that, of central importance to effective leadership, was the cooperation of others with a negotiated set of values and vision (Harris and Chapman, 2002). To lead change effectively, a school leader needs to be able to articulate their vision clearly and take others with them (Barber et al., 2010).

Culture

The term 'culture' applied in an educational context is a complex and important concept. Schein considers the basic essence of an organisation's culture to be 'the basic assumptions and beliefs that are shared by members of an organisation, that operate unconsciously', and that define, in a basic 'taken for granted' fashion, an organisation's view of itself and its environment (Schein, 1985:6).

Every institution operates differently as may be articulated as 'the way we do things around here' (Deal and Kennedy, 1982). A school also may have a view as to how it should be perceived in the external world. Culture is, thus, 'situationally unique' (Beare and Hogg, 2013) with a school's culture shaped by its history, context and those associated with it.

Understandings and definitions of school culture today generally encompass the beliefs, perceptions, relationships, attitudes and written and unwritten rules that shape and influence every aspect of how a school functions. The term also encompasses concrete issues such as the physical and emotional safety of students, the orderliness of classrooms and public spaces or the degree to which a school embraces and celebrates racial, ethnic, linguistic or cultural diversity.

A school culture is influenced from both conscious and unconscious perspectives, as well as by the values, interactions, and practices shaped by the institution's particular history. Students, parents, teachers, administrators and other staff members all contribute to the school's culture, as do other influences such as the community in which the school is located, the policies that govern how it operates or the principles upon which the school was founded.

The aim of any school leader or leadership team is to create a *positive culture* conducive to professional satisfaction, morale and effectiveness, as well as to student learning, fulfilment and wellbeing. A positive school culture might be characterised by:

- The recognition and praise for student and teacher effort.
- Relationships and interactions based on openness, trust, respect and appreciation.
- Staff relationships that are collegial, collaborative and productive, with the expectation of high professional standards.
- Students and staff members who feel emotionally and physically safe, as the school's policies and facilities promote student safety.
- School leaders, teachers and staff members who model positive, healthy behaviours for students.
- A situation where mistakes are seen as opportunities to learn and grow for both students and educators.
- Students who are consistently held to high academic expectations, with a majority of students meeting or exceeding those expectations.
- Important leadership decisions being made collaboratively with input from staff members, students and parents.
- Criticism that, when voiced, is constructive and well-intentioned, not antagonistic or self-serving.

- Educational resources and learning opportunities that are equitably distributed, for all students, including minorities and students with disabilities.
- All students having access to the academic support and services they may need to succeed.

For the cultural expectations identified to become part of any organisation there is a clear need for a leadership culture that accepts and promotes leadership as *a collective activity* to the benefit of the organisation as a whole. This might best be described as an interdependent leadership culture where all elements of the school system operate together for the common good.

Two opposing types have been identified, namely:

- A dependent leadership culture which suggest that *people in authority are totally responsible* for leadership and control the organisation.
- An independent leadership culture which promotes the idea that leadership emerges out of *individual expertise and heroic action*.

It may well be that in certain circumstances any one of three leadership cultures (interdependent, independent and dependent) might operate in an educational institution at any one time. Ideally, though, leaders should aim for an interdependent culture to encourage staff to join the intended joint endeavour.

Task 3.2 The dominant culture

What is the dominant culture in your organisation? Why is this the case? Can you think of any situations where this might change, where the other classifications listed are practised?

Once you have clarity around the current leadership culture you may wish, as an activity, to ask the question posed in Task 3.3.

Task 3.3 Positive impact

To what extent is organisational culture having a positive or negative impact on performance? Is the leadership culture helping to achieve the intended goals? Is everyone clear about what the organisational goals are and are these articulated clearly to all concerned?

Task 3.4 Critical evaluation

Read the vision statements and consider what a vision statement for the future might contain

Vision statement	Your thoughts
To create and enforce a clear and rigorous expectation to promote the fundamental British values of democracy, the rule of law, individual liberty and mutual respect and tolerance of those with different faiths and beliefs. (this statement is adopted from the DfES in the UK statement of British Values).	
Working together, achieving for all.	
To provide an intellectually challenging learning experience from which all pupils can benefit. This school is devoted to raising children's expectations and aspirations. Our principle objective is for each pupil to develop a deep interest in, and love for, learning. Pupils will be taught to apply this learning to the everyday world around them.	
Success through effort and determination.	

Reform

School culture has become a central concept in many efforts to change how schools operate and in the pursuit of improvements in educational results. While a culture is heavily influenced by its institutional history, culture also shapes the social patterns, habits, and dynamics that influence future behaviours. It is feasible that in some cases the culture of a school, if not framed in an ideology that embraces change and incorporates new ideas whilst honouring old traditions, may not be fit for purpose.

In the light of this a number of ways are suggested here as to how spaces of prescription might become spaces of negotiation and so improve school culture:

- Establish professional learning communities that encourage teachers to communicate, share expertise and work together more collegially and productively.
- Create a culture of professional engagement with presentations, seminars and learning experiences designed to engage staff.
- Involve students, even at a young age in committee membership, so that their view is valued.
- Celebrate success at all levels, not just in league table results. Make all staff feel that their contribution (on the sport field, in art displays, assemblies, etc.) is valued.

Newman Values

- We are **responsible for our own actions** and the impact they have upon others.
- We **respect the right of others** to learn and are prepared to learn ourselves.
- We actively **contribute to the life of the school** and the wider community.
- We **respect the faiths, cultures and values** of others in our community.
- We recognise that the purpose of **rules and laws are for the good of everyone**.
- We treat others **as we would like to be treated**.
- We actively encourage and promote the use of the **English language** by students at all times.

Figure 3.1 Newman values

- Survey students, parents and teachers about their experiences in the school, whilst hosting community forums that invite participants to share their opinions and recommendations for the school.
- Address issues as they arise, creating a leadership team comprising a representative cross-section of school administrators, teachers, students, parents and community members that oversee and lead school-improvement initiatives .

The commitment of the school to student rights, and to the use of English as the core language of communication, is clearly expressed here alongside a focus on the impact of actions on others. The school is acknowledged as a UNICEF rights-respecting institution; see Chapter 7 for more information about this and Chapter 8 which describes a special initiative at the school which is keeping pupils engaged in their schooling.

The National Professional Qualifications for standards for leadership covered in this chapter include:

Implementing successful change at a team and senior level.
Realising the benefits of collaborating with others, including teachers, teaching assistants, non-teaching staff, parents and carers.

References

Antonakis, J., Avolio, B.J. and Sivasubramaniam, N. (2004) Context and leader-ship: an examination of the nine-factor full-range leadership theory using the Multifactor Leadership Questionnaire. *The Leadership Quarterly*, 14, 261–295.

Barber, M., Whelan, F. and Clark, M. (2010) *Capturing the leadership premium: how the world's top school systems are building leadership capacity for the future.* London: McKinsey & Co.

Browne, E. and Kellsey Millar, D. (2019) Increasing student voice and empowerment through technology: not just listening to the voice of the learner but using their digital capabilities to benefit a whole college community. *Journal of Further and Higher Education*, 43 (10), 1433–1443.

Bush, T. (2007) Educational leadership and management: theory, policy, and practice *South African Journal of Education EASA*, 27 (3), 391–410.

Day, C. (2010) Professional development and reflective practice: purposes, processes and partnerships. *Pedagogy, Culture and Society*, 7 (2), 221–233.

Deal, T. and Kennedy, A. (1982) *Corporate cultures: the rites and rituals of corporate life*. Oxford: Oxford University Press.

Department for Education. (2014) A world-class teaching profession. https://www w.gov.uk/government/publications/a-world-class-teaching-profession (accessed 13.1.2018).

Durkheim, Émile. (2007) The rules of sociological method (1895). In Appelrouth, Scott, and Edles, Laura Desfor (eds.) *Classical and contemporary sociological theory: text and readings*. Thousand Oaks, CA: Pine Forge Press, pp. 95–102.

Harris, A. and Chapman, C. (2002) *Effective leadership in schools facing challenging circumstances*. Nottingham: National College for School Leadership.

Leithwood, R. and Riehl, M. (2013) What we know about successful school leadership. *American Research Association*, 2 (1), 235–254.

Northouse, P. (2004) *Leadership theory and practice*. London: SAGE.

Parsons, Talcott. (1991) A tintative outline of American values. In Roland Robertson and Bryan S. Turner (eds.) *Talcott parsons: theorist of modernity*. London: SAGE Publication, p. 1.

Schein, E. (1985) *Organizational culture and leadership*. New York: Josey Bass.

Smith, R. and Bell, D. (2015) *Management communication*. London: SAGE.

Southworth, G. (2011) Connecting Leadership and Learning. In Robinson, J. and Timperley, H. (eds.) *Leadership and Learning*. London: Sage, pp. 71–85.

Stoll, L. (2019) Creative leadership, the challenge of our times. https://www.research gate.net/publication/249014997_Creative_leadership.

Wilkins, A. (2017) Creating expert publics: a governmentality approach to school governance under neo-liberalism. In Courtney, S., McGinity, R. and Gunter, H. (eds.) *Educational leadership: professional practice in neoliberal times*. Routledge: London, pp. 97–110.

www.abingdonschool.org.uk

www.leyschool.org.uk

www.newmancollege.org.uk

PART II
Leadership with purpose

Leading a self-improving educational system

This chapter gives focus to two theoretical approaches to leadership which are closely aligned and interconnected in education practice in schools today. They are the theories of systems leadership and of distributed leadership. It is argued here that modern leadership approaches, where school leaders collaborate to support other leaders, and also to encourage the development of new leadership talent, work most effectively when functioning within a distributed leadership model. A report from the OECD highlights how countries such as England, Finland and Belgium have made systems leadership central to their school improvement strategies (OECD, 2019). In England this works through models of cooperation where headteachers work beyond their own schools to drive improvements across a region and disseminate what works as part of a system-wide strategy.

Across the globe, the 21st century is seeing rapid economic and social change. Social and population mobility, along with technological advances and an increased focus on schools to perform, mean that students today face very different challenges from their predecessors.

Together, these factors fundamentally alter the role of schools and school leaders and the challenges they face. In many countries school leaders now have more autonomy, but it is coupled with greater accountability. They must not only prepare all their students to participate successfully in the new global economy and society, they must take increasing responsibility for helping to develop other schools, their local communities and other public services. This means that school leaders must become systems leaders.

Systems leadership can build capacity in education; create shared expertise, facilities and resources; encourage innovation and creativity; improve leadership and spread it more widely; and provide skills support. Systems leadership rests on the belief that the collective sharing of skills, expertise and experience will create much richer and more sustainable opportunities for rigorous transformation than can ever be provided by isolated institutions. In times of major change, countries which have adopted a systems approach may find themselves in a better position to innovate whilst developing creative solutions to emerging problems.

What is systems leadership?

Education systems worldwide have identified the need for leaders to be agile in adapting to change and be focused on improving learning. This has created an approach to leadership known as 'systems leadership' which involves elements of a distributive leadership model if it is to work effectively. Distributed leadership is examined for the role it plays in supporting effective professional development and in initiating improvements in school and self, and thus in how it leads to wholescale school improvement.

Context

Research evidence has suggested that, after the quality of teaching, school leadership has the most impact on raising levels of student learning (Hattie, 2008). It has become accepted practice that when jurisdictions become focused on improving learner outcomes, they must systematically develop the expertise of school leaders (Leithwood and Seashore-Louise, 2011; Robinson, 2011). A systems approach to school leadership has been adopted by a number of countries including the UK, the USA, Australia and parts of New Zealand (Bush et al., 2010).

The approach

A system of school-to-school support, first used to help headteachers in American schools, and developed by the Department for Education in England, has resulted in more interschool collaborations with leaders of successful schools supporting those in less successful establishments.

The approach of school-to-school support is seen as particularly vital in addressing the challenges faced by underperforming schools, with outreach and community support also seen as part of the endeavour.

> When I describe systems leadership, what I mean is the way that groups of talented leaders work together to form plans and take decisions that have an impact on the outcomes and experiences of children in a whole community, and not just the school they attend.

David Carter – National Schools Commissioner www.systemsleadeship
https://schoolsweek.co.uk/building-an-education-system-on-collaboration-lea
dership-and-great-governance

Fullan (2005) has argued that systems leadership is imbued with a moral purpose designed to gain a better understanding of the factors that improve teaching and learning with the aim of changing situations where deprivation is still a predictor of educational failure. The ambition of systems leadership is to improve student learning and narrow the gaps between schools and the learners attending them. Systems Leaership then:

- encourages deeper engagement in the organisation of teaching, learning, curriculum and assessment in order to ensure that learning takes place.

And Systems leaders:

- support schools to become personal and professional learning communities, with relationships built across and beyond each school to provide a range of learning experiences and professional development opportunities.
- strive for equity and inclusion, acting on context and culture.
- understand that to activate change you have to engage at all levels of the classroom, the school and the system to inspire individuals and institutions to take small atomic steps towards powerful change.

There are a number of roles that leaders can take in this systems leadership approach, with leaders having the opportunity to be National Leaders of Education (NLEs), Local Leaders of Education (LLES) and School Improvement Partners (SIP) (this role is being phased out), or to take on the role as an executive head, where the leader of a successful school takes over the running of one that is deemed to be failing. All these roles fall within the definition of systems leadership where leaders work beyond their own school to support other schools. The National College defines the role as

> leaders who work within and beyond their individual organisations; sharing and harnessing the best resources that the system can offer to bring about improvement in their own and other organisations; and influencing thinking, policy and practice so as to have a positive impact on the lives and life chances of all children and young people.
>
> (National College 2, 2009:5) (Table 4.1)

Table 4.1 Improvement roles

Role	Professional Partners (PPS)	Local Leaders of Education (LLEs)	National Leaders of Education (NLEs)
Description	PPSs provide needs-based support and challenge.	LLEs provide coaching and mentoring to partner headteachers.	NLEs are outstanding school leaders who, with staff in their schools, provide additional leadership capacity to other schools.
	Help with the leadership and management of change.	They spend one day a week in other schools.	They offer additional leadership capacity where schools are in difficulty.
	Support headteachers to work with local and national children's service groups.	They address specific issues to build capacity and aid improvements.	They take over, where appropriate, underperforming schools and develop trusts, academies or chains of high performing organisations.
Typical time commitment	Up to 30 hours over two years per new headteacher.	Up to one day a week.	Can be a full-time role.

Source: NCSL (2015)

Case study 4.1 Cutteslowe School

John is the Head of Cutteslowe School in Oxfordshire, a school which was designated 'below the floor standard' (failing to reach the expected level) in 2014 when John took over, but identified in 2018 as one the ten most improved schools nationally. John has now been appointed as the executive head of two other schools in the area and he is working with the staff in these establishments to help them make improvements.

Case study 4.2 A rural school

James, appointed head of a rural school in Southern England following a Deputy Headship in a Northern Town, when interviewed, expressed concern about isolation:

> I am used to meeting with teachers from other schools, working collaboratively, having healthy competition and meeting to talk openly about new initiatives and different challenges. I know life at the top can be lonely but it is more than that. I miss the educational challenge that other colleagues can offer. I am currently trying to reach out to other schools to encourage shared planning meetings to prepare for curriculum change.

Leading with data

Using school data is a crucial way to model a systems approach to school leadership. Not only does the data help identify schools which would benefit from support for others, but it also allows leaders of learning to hone into the key areas that require attention. Data first became used as a key focus for reform during a project known as the 'London Challenge'.

This intervention in the English capital focused on school data to systematically challenge underperforming schools. Understanding school data was key to the success of this intervention, underpinned by the mantra of high expectation regardless of circumstance. The project focused on the 'smart' utilisation of data based on student outcome results and other data available not just to identify areas of weakness in the city's schools but also to identify 'positive outliers' and to target support. The London Challenge used consistent data-based criteria to identify underperforming schools and undertook pioneering work in the area of data benchmarking, used now more widely, within so-called 'families' of schools. Research indicated that the benchmarking of schools against the performance of other schools with similar characteristics was an important factor in the success of the programme (McAleavy et al., 2019). This use of benchmarking has now been further developed and advocated for all schools. Chapter 13 shows how this works in a range of different ways.

The London Challenge targeted whole districts within London identified as causes for concern, as well as specific underperforming schools – termed 'Keys to Success' (KTS) schools – across the city. The programme involved a range of school improvement initiatives, many of which made use of the expertise of the best practitioners and best schools, with an emphasis on school-to-school knowledge transfers.

Much of the school improvement activity centred on building relationships between high-performing and underperforming schools. This involved the sharing of expertise and training for leaders and teachers in underperforming schools, with the package of support for each school tailored and brokered by a London Challenge adviser. In particular, the programme developed the concept of systems leadership by pioneering the use of expert headteachers to mentor the headteachers of underperforming schools.

Research carried out some years after the London Challenge initiative funded by the Education Development Trust stated:

> In our view, London today constitutes a form of 'self-improving' school system. The key resource for school development is the collective expertise within the schools themselves rather than the work of external school improvement agencies. Consider that one of the greatest achievements of the London Challenge was that it built school-level capacity so that the momentum for improvement continued to build after the end of the intervention.
>
> (McAleavy et al., 2019:4)

Acknowledging the strength of a systems approach and highlighting the diverse nature of city schools, the authors of the report state that there is no single blueprint for how a successful London school should operate. However, lively professional discussion and the sharing of ideas promoted in a systems approach has fuelled a lively professional discourse in London about effective teaching and learning. One of the most impressive characteristics of the London system is a professional culture that involves high levels of both school-to-school competition and school-to-school collaboration, which requires a systems thinking approach.

What is systems thinking?

The ideas of systems thinking have grown from the concept of system dynamics. The idea is highly conceptual but can be applied to schools to support an understanding of practical school issues. The discipline of systems thinking teaches that in any social phenomenon it is important to look at the whole picture. In systems thinking the school is looked at as a system that is interconnected to different parts of life that intersect and influence each other (French and Bell, 1995:93). Schools exist as complex organisations with learners, educators, varying contexts, student learning processes and a range of components that affect learning. The core of systems lies in a view that sees interrelationships rather than linear cause–effect chains; and change as an ongoing process, not something to be achieved overnight.

Systems thinking starts with understanding the concept of feedback so that actions can reinforce or balance each other enabling educators to see the deeper patterns and interrelationships of change. This is the view expressed by Carter:

> Every school must give and receive support. Schools do not remain static for long. They are usually improving or declining and for that reason even the best schools in our education system will have pockets of practice that needs to improve. At the other end of the journey, a school that is in crisis will have some great practice, but maybe not enough of it. As a school moves through the improvement cycle, recognising the need to offer and accept support will become an important dimension of leadership thinking.
>
> (Carter, www.systemsleadership.com)

Table 4.2 outlines the components of systems leadership at a variety of operational levels (DfE, 2014).

Systems leaders need to have the ability to see the complexity of an organisation and see beyond the apparent to discover issues that might lurk beneath the surface. They will approach schools with 'fresh eyes' and be able to have an objective view of the issues that require attention. A systems leader will work effectively with existing staff to bring issues to the fore and discuss appropriate solutions in a dispassionate and objective fashion.

Table 4.2 Systems actions

Newman Values

---

* We are **responsible for our own actions** and the impact they have upon others.
* We **respect the right of others** to learn and are prepared to learn ourselves.
* We actively **contribute to the life of the school** and the wider community.
* We **respect the faiths, cultures and values** of others in our community.
* We recognise that the purpose of **rules and laws are for the good of everyone**.
* We treat others **as we would like to be treated**.
* We actively encourage and promote the use of the **English language** by students at all times.

Systems leaders need to encourage staff reflection and promote generative conversations which help those working in failing schools to think more openly about their challenges and hopefully find their own solutions. By encouraging reflection, the systems leader helps others to think about their thinking, challenge taken-for-granted assumptions and appreciate how mental models may limit progress. Reflection helps leaders to move away from a blame culture which may explain failure as being due to the local circumstances to embrace a 'can do' approach to change.

A further focus for the systems leader centres on shifting the collective focus from reactive problem-solving to co-creating the future. It requires a shift away from the negative to a 'can do' culture; effective systems leaders can envision a more positive future. They can see it and describe it, and can build a positive vision for the future. This typically happens gradually as leaders help people articulate their deeper aspirations and build confidence based on tangible accomplishments achieved together. This mirrors the atomic leadership approach with a gradual shift that involves building new visions and facing difficult truths about the present reality and learning how to use the tension between vision and reality to inspire truly new approaches.

Research carried out by Swaffield (2015) on the School Improvement Partners initiative in UK as a forerunner to the systems approach has highlighted a number of lessons for National and Local Leaders of Education. The school-to-school support relationship, she says, can be a tense one and needs to be built on reciprocity and respect, it being important that leaders provide both challenge and support. She highlights a risk in the systems approach where narrow measures of success around data are privileged. She reminds us that it is essential that systems leaders acknowledge the complex and interrelated factors around school performance and are willing to engage in a dialogue about learning, teaching and related matters rather than just data. For Swaffield, elements of challenge must be aligned to the expertise of the school leadership team and its values whilst also acknowledging the headteacher's expertise, readiness and needs. It is important that visiting systems leaders have credibility in the eyes of the other school leaders with appropriate expertise and experience.

Trust can never be a given and both parties in the relationship must work to create and maintain an effective working relationship. There should be no conflicts of interest, competing accountabilities or potential breaches of confidentiality. Time is necessary to develop this trust; understandings of context and purpose will require effort and mutual support if reflective conversations are to develop.

For the systems leader, well-developed interpersonal skills, personal commitment and professional attitudes and conduct will support the development of professional conversations essential for the growth of rapport and challenging conversation.

The following excerpt is taken from a governor visit report to a highly effective school. It describes the role played by the headteacher as a systems leader supporting other schools. First, though, it is important for John to be able to trust his leadership team and delegate to them, when he is supporting other institutions. He has been able to grow the capacity and confidence of his team to allow him to work outside his own institution, build the confidence of the leadership teams in other schools and develop a collaborative chain of school-to-school support across the schools he supports.

Case study 4.3 Governor visit

The leadership team at Thomas Reade Primary School consists of the Head, the Deputy Head (also with responsibility for Literacy), the Mathematics Co-ordinator and the Special Needs Co-ordinator. Other staff are invited to leadership meetings from time to time when specific issues might relate to their area of expertise. The structure, other than the leadership team, as described, is what might be defined as 'flat' rather than hierarchical. This, according to John, is deliberate, as for him hierarchical structures can be divisive, leading to resentment and unnecessary competition. However, John said that one thing he insists on is that all staff have the time to do their jobs effectively.

Distributed leadership according to John can only work when the leader has full confidence, trust and faith in those they work with. It is essential that heads can rely on their colleagues. In saying this John quoted an ex-headteacher he had worked under who said, 'You delegate or you disintegrate!' But, as John pointed out, there is a fine line between abdication and delegation and the head still has overall responsibility for everything that happens in the school. As John said, 'there is a fine line between being responsible, in supporting others to grow and empowering your staff whilst also knowing that you're the one who is overall in control'.

When asked about the evidence for effective distributed leadership John used the example of his role as a National Leader of Education (NLE) when supporting other schools in the region. This John would not be able to do with confidence if he did not trust his staff. Although he is never more than a short distance from the school and is always contactable by phone, John is able to

---

work with other heads knowing that the school is in good hands. John said he had confidence in the school's behaviour and welfare systems, that the school was offering an engaging curriculum and operating with solid, well-understood processes and systems. It was his trust in these systems and in his leadership team that enabled him to support other colleagues in local schools. This opportunity has also been afforded to other staff who have offered support in local schools in the area of literacy, assessment, writing, spelling and mathematics. The fact that the leadership team is also supporting local schools in difficulty is evidence of the trust placed in them by the head. It is also good continuing professional development (CPD) for those concerned, providing evidence of a school where staff are encouraged to grow and develop as future leaders.

International perspective

Finland is another country alongside England which has adopted a systems approach with success. Here it operates rather differently with a decentralised model based on distribution and co-operation with principals not only responsible for their own schools but also for their districts. There is shared management and supervision as well as evaluation and development of education planning. Finland was praised in the 'OECD Improving School Leadership' (2015) report for its innovative approach to distributing school leadership in a systemic way. Interestingly, principals in Finland are required by law to have been teachers themselves. Most continue to be engaged in classroom teaching for at least two to three hours – many up to 20 lessons per week. This has the benefit of giving them credibility among their teachers, enables them to remain connected to their children and ensures that pedagogical leadership is not merely rhetoric but a day-to-day reality.

Research by the OECD into systems approaches has identified that principals from Finland are not subject to the number, pace and range of reforms demanded by external government: 'unlike other countries, we do not have to spend our time responding to long lists of government initiatives that come from the top' (OECD, 2015).

One outcome of this model is that distributed leadership is an endemic feature of Finnish schools, rather than something which individual actors assign or delegate to others as a way to get policy implemented. In the conception of key writers in the field, distributed leadership here is not a set of practices initiated and handled by principals or senior officials. Leadership, rather, is already distributed throughout the culture and organisation of the schools (Crowther and Danielson, 2002; Spillane, 2006).

53

In Finish society principals and teachers are regarded as a 'society of experts'. In one municipality, the upper secondary school was described as 'an organisation of experts who know their subjects and teach them well'.

In the words of a member of the National Principals' Council

> Working in schools is easy because we don't have principals acting like a big manager. It's more like a society of experts. We really share things because principals also have pedagogical understanding and that's important. They have to know how to do the job and they still teach during the week. You really know how the work is. You are not just sitting higher and acting like a big manager.

The operation of this 'society of experts' is seen as being neither authoritarian, nor especially academic, but a cooperative (OECD, 2015).

Another model is adopted in Canada where retired lead teachers are employed to work with new leaders in their schools to offer challenge and support, bringing their experience to influence the decision-making processes applied by those new to a leadership role (Whiteley et al., 2017).

Linking systems leadership to traditional leadership theory

The concentration of systems leaders in the English model on data, feedback, evaluation and decisions made in an organisation match the ideas of transformational theory where transformational leaders working in a climate of transparency present staff with data and information to help staff make better school decisions to improve all aspects of the school including teaching and learning. For systems leadership to be effective, leaders need to distribute a range of their tasks to others in their leadership team, thus freeing up time and opportunity for headteachers to support other leaders.

Systems leadership has become a central concept in the operation of effective schooling with effective leaders being encouraged to share their expertise to support other leaders. Systems leadership is intended to promote a culture of trust, one which faces problems and addresses them whilst supporting staff members to collaborate and engage in productive professional discourse. A systems leadership approach is seen as one that is conducive to improvement, where reform becomes exponentially easier to achieve.

The following describe a few representative examples of common ways that schools, using a systems leadership philosophy, may attempt to improve their culture:

- Establishing professional learning communities that encourage teachers to communicate, share expertise and work together more collegially and productively.

- Providing presentations, seminars and learning experiences designed to educate staff and students about bullying and reduce instances of bullying.
- Creating events and educational experiences that honour and celebrate the racial, ethnic and linguistic diversity of the student body, such as hosting cultural events and festivals, exhibiting culturally relevant materials throughout the school, inviting local cultural leaders to present to students or making explicit connections between the diverse cultural backgrounds of students and what is being taught in history, social studies and literature courses.
- Establishing an advisory programme that pairs groups of students with adult advisors to strengthen adult–student relationships and ensure that students are well-known and supported by at least one adult in the school.
- Surveying students, parents and teachers about their experiences in the school, and hosting community forums that invite participants to share their opinions about and recommendations for the school and its programmes.
- Creating a leadership team comprising a representative cross-section of school administrators, teachers, students, parents and community members that oversees and leads a school-improvement initiative.
- Working with colleagues in other schools, and helping them to learn from your experience whilst advising them on the benefits of a systems approach.

(DfE, 2010)

What remains to be seen is whether ideas of systems leadership, as discussed in this chapter, are agile enough to address the current challenges. The pressures of aiming for continuous improvement can be great, causing anxiety and tensions which might lead to a breakdown in the stable operation of the school with staff shortages, illness and uncertainty.

Gunter (2010) has cautioned against systems leadership on the basis of the added pressure it places on school leaders. Indeed, school leadership is a complex activity and the responsibilities of leaders have increased considerably in recent times. Headteachers are responsible for student learning whilst also required to support the development of their staff (see Chapter 10). They are required to take on board community issues and connect with parents, governors and local leaders. Resource leadership is another complex part of the role with responsibility for finances, buildings, technology, maintenance and health and safety. Safeguarding and reporting issues to external bodies, whilst addressing the needs of growing numbers of children with additional needs, add another dimension of complexity. So do responding to a plethora of policy change (see Chapter 5) whilst improving student achievement, balancing competing interests, strategising and implementing change. One such policy change includes the requirement to demonstrate effective distributed leadership, now included as part of the 2019 Inspection Framework for English Schools.

So, what is distributed leadership?

Distributed models of leadership, essential in addressing the complexities of modern-day leadership, start from the belief that the act of leading, showing direction, can occur through a number of individuals and across an organisation. As a model that advocates democratic decision-making it acknowledges the interdependence of all work in the organisation and allows for multiple voices to be heard. Distributed leadership allows a school leader to show trust in their colleagues and prepare individuals for future roles, and permits the sharing of authority and responsibility.

Distributed leadership theory encourages the involvement of teachers and stakeholders in decision-making; it allows leadership to become an aggregate of behaviours that can be adopted by more than one person. It permits a shift in authority and responsibility away from one person to encourage participation and empowerment.

Where distributed leadership is working well, colleagues will share data, share a collective responsibility and be aware collectively of the facts and figures that will impact on student performance and limit the culture of improvement. With shared knowledge a collective responsibility develops for issues such as resource management and financial regulation.

Teachers see themselves as interconnected, not isolated; they take ownership for problems and actively share common values, collaboratively building towards collective beliefs and working together for the benefit of the whole school.

Where models of distributed leadership exist, leadership becomes more of a collective achievement based on the contribution of every participant. Decision-making can be expanded to take in a wider range of views and perspectives. And the leaders who operate a distributed model are confident leaders, ones who can see the complexity of the challenges they face but are prepared to acknowledge the professional skills and knowledge of their staff and allow for networks of support to grow and develop without feeling personally threatened in their role.

Distributed leadership can create an environment where democratic decision-making can thrive. Where staff collaborate and exchange ideas, and solve problems collegiately (Bush et al., 2010). Here individual qualities can be developed, sometimes for a few selected staff in a 'restricted 'model (Bush, 1995) or a broader sense as a 'pure' model (Bush et al., 2010:52) where responsibility is shared across whole organisations.

Given the complexity of the world we live in and the need for schools to adapt to address multiple challenges in an environment where VUCA dominates, a distributed model of leadership is essential, particularly in environments where systems approaches are placing more pressures on the time of already busy headteachers.

Task 4.1 School research

Consider a school other than your own and discover as much about it as you can. Look in school league tables, inspection reports. You can do this whether you work England or elsewhere in the world, but in the English system your source of information will be the DfE website, the school website, the latest OfSTED report and the Education Endowment Foundation's (EEF) Families of Schools Databases. Analyse the performance data for this school looking at trends over time. Consider how much confidence you can have in the data and then develop a communications plan as if you had been appointed as a Local Leader of Education to work with this school. Identify the key strengths and weaknesses and consider how your first meeting with the school's leadership team might progress if the meeting is to establish the ground rules for a good working relationship.

Systems leadership, with its focus on data and performance, is not without its critics. Sergiovanni (2005) reminds us of the dimensions of school life which are more than adherence to data and systems, he refers to a 'life world', where schools need to have an existence beyond a feverish adherence to examination results. It is worth noting that the following NPQ criteria urge prospective leaders to think about school success other than in terms of data, and this is encouraging – something perhaps to read now?

The criteria for the achievement of the National Professional Qualifications for Leadership addressed in this chapter are:

Put in place systems, processes and structures which facilitate knowledge transfer and shared best practice with and beyond the school.

Ensure data collected is necessary, proportionate and manageable for staff.

Reduce variation within schools and against comparative schools by improving pupil progress, attainment and behaviour.

Analyse performance data to identify causes of variation within a school and against comparative schools.

Think about the school in terms of achievements other than those linked to the available data. What is good about this school in terms of the way it encourages young people to be active and moral citizens of the future?

Design and implement change across schools.

References

Bush, T. (1995) *Theories of education management.* London: SAGE.

Bush, T, Bell, L. and Middlewood, D. (eds.) (2010) *The principles of educational leadership and management.* London: SAGE.

Carter, D. (2015) National Schools Commissioner. www.systemsleadeship https://schoolsweek.co.uk/building-an-education-system-on-collaboration-leadership-and-great-governance

Crowther, P. and Danielson, M. (2002) *Teacher leadership: an assessment framework.* London: Heinemann.

Department for Education. (2010) *The importance of teaching.* Schools White Paper 2010, Norwich, Stationery Office.

Department for Education. (2014) *System leadership in action.* Norwich: The Stationery Office. London: DfE.

French, W. and Bell, C. (1995) *Organization development: behavioural science interventions for organization improvement,* 5th ed. Oxford: Pearson's.

Fullan, M. (2005) *Leadership and school reform.* London: SAGE.

Gunter, H. (2010) A sociological approach to educational leadership. *British Journal of Sociology of Education,* 31 (4), 519–527.

Hattie, J. (2008) *High impact leadership.* London: ACSD.

Leithwood, K. and Seashore-Louis, K. (2011) *Linking leadership to student learning.* San Francisco, CA: Jossey Bass.

McAleavy, T., Elwick, A. and Hall-Chen, A. (2019) *Sustaining success: high performing government schools in London.* London: Education Development Fund.

National College of School Leadership. (2009) *Leadership report 2.* Nottingham: NCSL.

National College of School Leadership. (2015) *Systems leadership.* Nottingham: NCSL.

OECD. (2015) *Improving school leadership. Vol. 2: Case studies on systems leadership.* Paris: OECD. ISBN: 978-92-64-03308-5.

OECD. (2019) *Education at a glance.* Paris: OECD.

Robinson, L. (2011) *Student centred leadership.* San Francisco, CA: Jossey Bass.

Sergiovanni, J. (2005) *Leadership and excellence in schooling: excellent schools need freedom within boundaries.* London: ASDA.

Spillane, J.P. (2006) *Distributed leadership.* San Francisco, CA: Jossey-Bass.

Swaffield, S. (2015) Support and challenge for school leaders: headteachers' perceptions of school improvement partners. *Journal of Educational Management Administration and Leadership,* 43 (1), 234–245.

Whiteley, G., Domaradzki, L., Costa, A. and Muller, P. (2017) *Dispositions of leadership: the effects on student learning and school culture.* Vancouver: Rowman & Littlefield Publishers.

Emerging school associations
The English story

Focus has been given to the challenges facing education today in the VUCA world. In the current times of change, different forms of school organisation are emerging and this is particularly prevalent in the English system where, under the mantra of achieving excellence, new forms of schooling have developed. The majority of schools in England are no longer run by local authorities (or 'districts' as they are named in other jurisdictions), but by business organisations, international companies, charities and church diocesan groups in what has been named the academy movement. This chapter identifies the types of schooling available in the UK and asks what this might mean for leaders aspiring to take on the challenge of leading in a school that might have different organisational arrangements from the one in which they were educated or once worked.

 How many schools are there in the UK?

At the time of writing there are a total of 32,770 schools in the UK. This figure consists of:

- 3,714 nurseries or early-learning centres.
- 20,832 primary schools.
- 19 middle schools (a model of schooling for 9–13 year olds, once quite common but now in decline).
- 4,188 secondary schools.
- 2,408 independent schools.
- 1,257 special schools.
- 352 pupil referral units (PRUs).

(Department for Education; Welsh Government; Scottish Government;
Northern Ireland Department of Education, 2018–19)

In addition to the classification of primary, secondary and independent, as used earlier, there are variations of schools within these groups giving a smorgasbord of variety in UK schooling. Given the additional complexity, selecting an appropriate school for your child must be a nightmare for the concerned parent. The following is a list of all the types of school available in the English system!

State boarding schools.
Special educational needs schools.
City technology colleges.
Faith schools.
Free schools.
Community schools.
Converter academies.
Multi-academy trusts (MATs).
Sponsored academies with one sponsor, sponsoring only one school, so not part of
    a MAT.
Voluntary aided schools.
Grammar schools

Less than ten years ago the landscape for schools would have been very different with a range of new school arrangements now present which parents have to grapple with. This chapter attempts to present a balanced picture emerging from the growing number of MAT schools, but first some thoughts about what this complex picture of school type means for the prospective leader.

Previously, if you were searching for a leadership position in the non-independent sector, it was guaranteed that one school would be managed much the same as another, with the local authority providing funding and having responsibility for certain areas such as children with special needs, newly qualified teachers (NQTS), continuing professional development (CPD) and the monitoring of school finance. Now, when applying for a leadership position, there is much more preparation to do such as confirming the type of school, who might be the sponsor, how that sponsor operates, whether the school adheres to national pay scales, the philosophy of the school and where decisions about leadership really rest. This point is expanded upon later.

What does the changing landscape mean for those interested in a leadership position?

Given the multiple types of school and the range of sponsors or local authorities responsible for them, it is worth doing some research before applying to work in an educational establishment. Of course, not everyone has the choice of where they

Table 5.1 Pre-appointment questions

Who makes the key decisions about the school?

What role does the sponsor or local authority take?

Whose values are included in leadership decisions?

What are the patterns of interaction between and among individuals who work and study in the institutions?

What are the opportunities for enquiry, critique and dialogue? Who initiates this? Who participates?

What does critique look like? Are some topics taboo? If so, which ones?

What are the assumed norms, beliefs and values? Are they educationally sound? Can you commit to them, or know how you might wish to change them?

How are the norms, values and beliefs communicated?

What is the stated school mission and ethos (see Chapter 3)? Does this ethos match with your ideology? Does the school mission align with your ambitions for the school?

How are new ideas introduced? Who has the opportunity to suggest change and how might this be done?

Who is included and excluded, including learners, and how are decisions made? Who is included in the process and when?

Who has responsibility if things are not working properly?

Who has access to the leadership team and/or the chief executive of the MAT?

Who makes financial decisions? Who deploys staff and who deals with publicity?

(Adapted and extended from work by Morrison, 2009).

work, and in what type of school, but it is worth reading as much as you can about your potential future employer before you apply for a job with them. Some key questions to ask when taking a leadership position are listed in Table 5.1. Some may be answered prior to an interview through investigation of the school website, while others may need to explore during the interview process.

Once you are hired, it may be wise to take initially the atomic leadership approach with small-scale interventions introduced gradually. Borrowed from Brighouse (1991), Table 5.2 below presents some positive aspirations for leaders to follow on a daily basis.

Background information

As mentioned earlier in this chapter, traditionally state schools (those funded by the state and not independent of government funding) were managed by the local authority which employed a cadre of staff to manage school transport, allocate school

Table 5.2 Leadership aspirations

- Be cheerful and optimistic, stay in charge of anger and conflict.
- Be welcoming and ready to be enthusiastic, engage dissidents and resist pointless struggles for power and position.
- Be a good listener – maintain courtesy and respectful behaviour irrespective of status or position.
- Achieve a number of short-term objectives to pave the way for higher goals.
- Keep fit, keep healthy, let go of guilt.
- Have a considered view and approach to the use of your time.
- Never forget that there is more than one option.
- Celebrate what others achieve whilst being able to take the blame when things go wrong.
- Be open to managing change and living in a changing environment.
- Be clear on your educational philosophy, be committed to making a difference and set a personal example in all interactions with staff, students, governors and external bodies.

places, advise headteachers on finance, resources and legal matters whilst also offering CPD. This took the form of the advisory service, with advice and training offered to newly qualified teachers and those working with students with special needs.

In the 1980s schools were encouraged to 'opt out' of local authority control and manage their own budget. The title 'academy' was later given to high-achieving schools which wanted independence and could demonstrate their ability to deliver a quality education system. When first established the term 'academy' denoted a high-achieving school, to be seen by others as an example of excellence.

In 2010, when the government in the UK changed its political affiliation, the academy movement was created, as a redefinition of the term. This movement has had a major reforming impact on the structural organisation of schools in the UK and has marked for some the quasi-privatisation of the education system with companies, charities, private enterprises, the church and independent schools all permitted to take over the running of schools. 'Academies are established and managed by sponsors from a wide range of backgrounds' (PricewaterhouseCoopers 2008:22).

There are now a number of academies operating with external partners in what have been classified as Multi-academy trusts (MATs). MATs and individually sponsored academies receive their funding directly from government, cutting out the need for local authority support and advice. Local authorities retain their responsibility for the allocation of school places, transport and the training and support of NQTs and for students with designated learning difficulties. At the time of writing, there are 1,170 multi-academy trusts in England that manage at least two schools. Twenty-nine MATs have 26 or more schools, 85 have between 12–25 schools and 259 have 6–11 schools. The majority of MATs – 598 – have five or fewer schools (DfE, 2020).

Sponsored academies are unique among English schools in that their governance is controlled by external sponsors. A variety of organisations with different cultures

Table 5.3 The academy movement

- Academies receive their funding directly from the government, rather than through local authorities like other state funded schools.
- There are two types: Converter academies (those deemed to be performing well that have converted to academy status) and sponsored academies (mostly underperforming schools changed to academy status and run by sponsors).
- A comparison of the most recent OfSTED grade of each type of school shows that converter academies are the most likely to be good and outstanding while sponsored academies are more likely than maintained schools to be graded as 'requires improvement' or 'inadequate'. But this is to be expected as converters are high performing, and sponsored low performing, to begin with.
- Evidence on the performance of academies compared to local authority schools is mixed, but on the whole suggests there is no substantial difference in performance. State-funded schools (including primary, secondary and special schools for pupils with special educational needs) fall into two main groups:
  - Maintained schools – where funding and oversight is through the local authority. These are the majority of schools and are mostly either community schools (where the local authority employs the school's staff and is responsible for admissions) or foundation schools, where the school employs the staff and has responsibility for admissions.
  - Academies – where funding and oversight is from the Department for Education (DfE) via the Education and Skills Funding Agency. They are run by an academy trust which employs the staff. Grammar schools are state-funded selective secondary schools. Most of these (140 out of 163) are now academies (www.dfe.gov.uk/schoolsbytype).

and ethos have set up academies and now operate MATs. They might be characterised as:

- Philanthropic sponsors.
- High-achieving school sponsors.
- Multi-academy trust sponsors.
- Group sponsors, some of which might have a religious affiliation.

Table 5.3 sets out in bullet points some key points to remember about academies.

Freedoms offered to academies

Academies are run by academy trusts and, rather like independent schools, do not have to follow the national curriculum, although the external pressure of examination tests does ensure a certain level of automatic compliance with academies being required to provide a curriculum that is 'balanced and broadly based' (DfE, 2014). Academies tend to have greater freedom to set their own term times and admissions, although this is a complex area with the Timpson Review (2014) recording some concern over the number of exclusions from some academies particularly prior to the onset of national tests: 'it cannot be right to have a system where some schools could stand to improve their performance and finances through exclusions' (Timpson, 2019:12).

Academies still have to follow the same rules on special educational needs being bound by the Children and Families Act (2014). And, where they use their right to exclude pupils, they should follow the same rules as other state schools, and are required to provide a curriculum that includes English, mathematics and science.

A 2014 survey of academies by DfE found that 87% say they are now buying services previously provided by the local authority from elsewhere, 55% have changed the curriculum, 8% have changed the length of their school day and 4% have changed the school terms. Whilst various other changes were also reported, it is not clear to what extent these are a direct result of academy conversion rather than changes that would have taken place regardless. A similar survey by think tank Reform and education body SSAT found slightly different percentages, but concluded that in terms of providing 'something new and different to the education that went before […] academies remain an unfinished revolution' (www.dfe.gov.uk/schoolsbytype).

And again, a reminder that academies fall into two main categories:

* **Sponsored academies** – these have sponsors such as businesses, universities, other schools, faith groups or voluntary groups, who have majority control of the academy trust. Most, but not all, sponsored academies were previously underperforming schools that became academies in order to improve their performance.
* **Converter academies** – these don't have sponsors, and are schools previously assessed as 'performing well' that have 'converted' to academy status.

It is important to focus on some of the good news coming out of sponsored academies, many of which form part of a multi-academy trust (MAT), the largest of which currently consists of 66 schools. One interesting MAT, the Harris Federation MAT, currently consists of 48 primary and secondary schools around London, is sponsored by Philip Harris – Lord Harris of Peckham – and provides education for more than 36,000 students. It has gained media attention because the rapper Stormsy, who attended one of the Harris Federation Schools, has set up a foundation to help black students offering them scholarships if they apply and go to Cambridge.

This same MAT held a conference for 4,500 staff and students in the Excel Centre in London. Students from Harris Academy Beckenham compere the conference and a school choir of 150 students sang. There was an award ceremony with prizes in leadership categories such as 'Transforming Young Lives' and 'Leader of Initial Teacher Education'.

Another positive story relates to Beacon Academy, operating as part of the Wellsprings Academy Trust, where school exclusions are a thing of the past and OfSTED have praised the school for its culture of inclusion and compassionate leadership. The following case study offers more detail.

Case study 5.1 Beacon Academy

Headteacher of Beacon Academy Jason Thurley has been praised for 'on rolling' excluded pupils from the area.

Jason Thurley, headteacher at Beacon Academy near Grimsby, leads a school which accepts pupils that other local schools cannot manage. One pupil excluded for taking a £1 potato gun into school was accepted at Beacon aged 11 and is now a year 10 sports leader who helps organise cross-country championships. Thurley says of the school philosophy, 'We batter them with kindness'.

Almost one-fifth of the year 10s were 'managed moves', meaning their school excluded them or was about to and had asked other heads to take them in. The rest arrived from pupil referral units, moved into the area, or, like the head boy, had previously been home educated. One pupil arrived after trying to burn down an art block. Another was rejected by three schools before Beacon took him.

Taking as many vulnerable pupils as possible – and never excluding them – is core to Thurley's mission in this deprived coastal corner of north-east Lincolnshire. His stance reflects the values of the sponsor, the Wellspring academy trust.

Since the trust was formed in 2017 not one student has been permanently excluded at any of its 20 mainstream schools. The trust also has six alternative provision and three special educational needs schools, and bills itself as promoting inclusion and compassionate leadership as its central philosophy (www.beaconacademy.org).

The school has to be admired, and indeed OfSTED has acknowledged that, despite some low results in external SAT tests, the leadership and management of this school is beyond reproach. This has been achieved by establishing special teams of staff concerned with the safety and wellbeing of the many vulnerable pupils:

Leadership of this area is strong and there is a dedicated, well-trained team which supports vulnerable pupils. Staff in this team make referrals in a swift and timely fashion. They show persistence and determination in the way that they ensure that pupils quickly get the help that they need. Records are detailed and of a high quality. (OfSTED, 2014)

MATs do not always attract good publicity. This was apparent in a BBC TV series which saw a headteacher resign because he could not accept some of the cuts in staffing expected of him by his MAT executive leaders. The series, which looked at a number of schools in South Gloucestershire (www.bbc.co.uk.news-england-gloucest

ershire46458574), shows the conflict that can develop between MAT executive leaders and school leaders where leadership styles and ambitions do not agree. There is also evidence, in the same region, of the worst performing school in England for pupil progress where one MAT leader had to be replaced.

What is clear is that MATs are receiving mixed reviews and also, depending on the sponsor, may present a completely different culture and philosophy than a prospective leader might have met before. It is vital, if applying for a post in a MAT, that you 'do your homework' and be clear that you can commit to the philosophy of the lead organisation and work with it.

It has been shown that headteachers and middle leaders who cannot follow the approach advocated by their MAT bosses will struggle to survive as leaders in an academy school (BBC documentary, Thornbury School, 2019).

In the same region, Gloucester Academy has transferred from its position as part of the White Horse Federation to becoming a member of the Greenshaw Learning Trust showing that government will not allow poor performance to go unnoticed with government intervention impacting on the organisational leadership of schools at the highest levels.

Criticism of MATs can also be found from sources such as OfSTED where concerns have been expressed about 'off rolling', a practice where students who are not likely to achieve a reasonable score in the School Assessment Tests (SATs) are excluded from the school.

The Audit Commission has also highlighted its concern about the high salaries paid to MAT Executive Leaders at a time when teachers' salaries have been either frozen or put under threat. Alongside this criticism OfSTED reported in early 2020 that 443 schools have failed to show signs of improvement despite regular inspection (The Guardian Newspaper, www.guardianeducation.schoolsstilfailing). And, despite one of the largest academy trusts being forced to relinquish ten of its schools for failing to make improvements, government ministers are still strongly advocating conversion to academy status (www.dfe/academysuccess.org.uk).

Economic and organisational benefits of MATs

One of the arguments in favour of MATs and advocated in an article by Evans from the Frogmore Association is their ability to pool resources, support one another and share best practices whilst encouraging collaboration. This centralist approach, it is argued, allows for the streamlining of documents and processes to reduce workload, improve pupil outcomes and drive consistency and efficiency (Evans, 2019). The Frogmore Association advocates the use of centralised information and communication systems to reduce bureaucracy as well as save money by:

- Removing redundant subscriptions to multiple software tools.
- Enabling comparisons of performance data across schools so that pockets of stronger and weaker teaching practice can be identified more easily, and support deployed more effectively.
- Allowing for the identification of good practice which can be, through coaching and inhouse training, disseminated across schools in the MAT.
- Ensuring resources can be easily shared between schools via one intranet system.
- Saving manpower on administration and HR task by centralising policies and procedures.
- Reducing teacher workload which has a positive impact on staff retention and morale, lowering the rate of staff turnover and absence (potentially reducing recruitment and cover costs).

This list is particularly interesting as it indicates the likelihood of high levels of central control if school leaders work in a large MAT. Leadership in this scenario becomes much more negotiated and based on models of limited power and authority, with decisions made centrally and based on data. Data-based decisions have impacted on education in a number of ways, creating leadership styles which become low on influence and highly prescribed by external evidence (Browne and Raynor, 2015). A prescriptive approach can lead to additional pressures for those taking leadership roles in MAT schools. It may be easier to lead where the data appears to provide the answers, but the lack of space for personal interpretation and justification may be difficult for others.

> **Task 5.1 Leading a MAT**
>
> Think about what working as a leader in a MAT might mean: What will be the key areas to consider on a day-to-day basis? Think about external audit, your colleagues, your approach to leadership and how you will operate within the MAT environment where executive MAT leaders may well hold you to account for your leadership on a weekly basis.

The DfE workforce challenge report identifies MATs as having further benefits of reducing workload. Again, centralised systems are advocated for planning and resource management with lesson plans and schemes of work, along with exemplary materials and teaching resources shared across schools. Evans again describes this system as creating 'one source of truth with teaching and learning materials shared to help raise standards' (Frogmore, 2019).

Working in a collective of schools alongside other leaders and reporting to an executive leader, which is the structural organisation prevalent in most MATs, will require what has been described as authentic leadership. This requires the ability to respond to the demands of MAT leaders whilst also maintaining the respect of your staff if difficult decisions, such as school restructuring and cost savings, are requested. Authentic leadership is needed to gain the trust of those you work with, so as to be known as genuine and honest so that people can follow your requests. The authentic leader will be able to have compassion and empathy, and will be able to judge the impact of decisions on those they work with. A consistent approach is essential, offering balance and fairness with no demonstration of favouritism. This requires self-knowledge and a clear set of values that will be respected and followed by others (Irvine and Reger, 2006; George, 2003).

The authentic leader will take ownership of mistakes and be prepared to challenge decisions by taking issues further up the leadership chain. They will question the current status quo or defend their people or processes. The authentic leader will know their own values and have a clear view of what is right. They will aim to always do things for the right reason and in the right way and be able to help others navigate change in times of uncertainty.

Federations

Another form of collaborative working can be seen in the federation approach. This involves a collection of schools working in partnership and is often focused on achieving more than any one single institution could do. Federations include partnerships on curriculum design and specialisms, including sharing curricular innovation to respond to key challenges, 14-to-19 consortia, behaviour and hard-to-place students. The partnership or federation may work collaboratively at multiple levels, with classroom assistants, teachers, subject leaders and administrators. While many partnerships are 'soft' organisational collaboratives, others have moved to 'harder', more formalised arrangements (to develop stronger mechanisms for joint governance and accountability) or education improvement partnerships (to formalise the devolution of responsibilities and resources from their local authority). The following issues require consideration:

- Choosing to lead and improve a school in extremely challenging circumstances, and building a culture of success to sustain high levels of added value, is challenging.
- Partnering another school facing difficulties and improving it, either as an executive head of a federation or as the leader of a more informal improvement, can be very rewarding.

(Hargreaves et al., 2015)

Task 5.2 Authentic leadership

Consider the requirements of authentic leadership. Do you have the right skills and abilities to lead a school that is part of a MAT?

Task 5.3 Evaluate your leadership style

Rank each of the following characteristics and strategies according to the following criteria:

- A = Well-established, confident, consistent usage
- B = Present but not consistently or confidently used
- C = An area for development

Characteristics of high-performing leaders

1. Focus on achievement
   Strong emphasis on achievement and closing the gap.
   A genuine focus on progress for all.
   A commitment to improving performance.
   A relentless focus on teaching and learning.
2. Consistency
   Public and explicit expectations and norms.
   Established routines, systems and procedures.
   Monitoring and review – evidence-based intervention.
   Prevention rather than cure.
   Leaders as models of consistency.
3. Effective relationships
   Focus on quality relationships.
   Recognition of vulnerable pupils' needs.
   Positive behaviour.
   Mutual respect between pupils and staff.
   Leaders focus on care and wellbeing.
4. Commitment
   Help and support over and above formal requirements.
   Ensuring progress and success for all pupils.
   Creative and innovative strategies to secure improvement.
   Team leaders focused on good and outstanding performance.

5. High expectations
   High aspirations and the norm.
   Leaders set and model high standards.
   High expectations in every aspect of school life.
6. Modelling
   Leading by example.
   Committed, passionate and driven.
   Sharing good practice.
   The organisation is a reflection of the leader.
7. Monitoring
   Accountability is clear and understood.
   Explicit and agreed criteria and protocols.
   Monitoring of teacher effectiveness.
   Evidence-based review and decision-making.
8. Dialogue
   Focus on students and learning.
   Open, transparent and supportive.
   Continuous, formal and informal.
   Focus on improving practice, sharing strategies.
9. Structures and systems
   Meticulous and detailed planning.
   Detailed planning and infrastructure.
   Sophisticated student data systems.
   Reinforcement of consistent approaches.
10. Retention of staff
    High trust; shared leadership.
    Empowerment.
    Positive regard.
11. Professional development
    Focused on learning and teaching.
    Primarily in-house.
    Leaders as lead learner and developer.
12. Team culture
    Focused on success and progress.
    Open, questioning and challenging.

This review is an opportunity to reflect on the extent to which you or your chosen leader meet these criteria for effective leadership. All judgements are inevitably subjective – this review is most likely to be useful when perceptions are compared and contrasted and used as the basis for shared review, discussion and learning conversations.

Totals	1	2	3	4	5	6	7	8	9	10	11	12
A												
B												
C												

Task 5.4 Self-evaluation

What are your areas of greatest strength and consistency?
Which areas need reinforcement?
Which areas are significant developmental needs?
How do your perceptions compare with those of colleagues?
Test your perceptions against those of your colleagues.

Please explore the implications of your scoring:

Self: What do they mean for you in your role as a leader? Are you clear and confident about the new leadership strategies you might need to employ?
School: What do you see as the most significant issues for your school to come to terms with?
System: What are the implications for your relationships with other schools, the local authority, other agencies and the wider community – notably parents?

Self   *School*   *System*

Task 5.5 Evaluation of your organisation

Evaluate your organisation's effectiveness in terms of partnership working. Who do you work with? Is the relationship productive and is there room for improved relationships?

Based on reading this chapter what are your views about applying for a more senior role than the one you now have?

The competencies for the National Professional Qualification for Leadership covered in this chapter are:

Identify a range of local and national partners that can support school improvement.

Realise the benefits of collaborating with others, including teachers, teaching assistants and non-teaching staff, other schools parent/careers and other organisations.

References

Brighouse, T. (1991) *What makes a good school.* Stafford Education Press.

Browne, E. and Rayner, S. (2015) Managing leadership in University reform: data-led decision-making, the cost of learning and deja vu? *Educational Management Administration and Leadership,* 43 (2), 290–307.

Department for Education and Skills. (2014) *The children and families act.* Norfolk: Her Majesties Stationery Office. https://inews.co.uk/news/education/school-bbc-documentary-crisis-classroom

Department for Education and Skills. (2020) Transparency data open academies, free schools, studio schools and UTCs Information on all academies, free schools, studio schools and university technical colleges (UTCs) open in England, and those in the process of opening. Published 20 March 2014 Last updated 7 August 2020

Evans, L. (2019) *The value of multi academy trusts.* London: The Frogmore Association.

George, B. (2003) *Authentic leadership: rediscovering the secrets to lasting value.* San Francisco, CA: Jose Bass.

Hargreaves, A., Halász, G. and Pont, B. (2015) *System leadership in action.* London: Penguin.

Irvine, D. and Reger, J. (2006) *The authentic leader.* Sandford: DC Press.

Morrison, M. (2009) *Leadership and learning matters of social justice.* London: Information Age Publishing.

Office for Standard in Education and Development (OfSTED). (2014) *Comparing school performance data*. London: HMSO.

Price, Waterhouse Coopers. (2008) *Emerging school associations: the English project*. London: PWC.

Timpson, R. (2019) Timpson review of school exclusion. https://assets.publishing.serv ice.gov.uk/.../807862/Timpson.

www.bbc.co.uk.news-england-gloucestershire46458574

www.guardianeducation.schoolsstilfailing (accessed 15th May, 2020).

www.beaconacademy.org.uk (accessed 15th May, 2020).

https://inews.co.uk/news/education/school-bbc-documentary-crisis-classroom (accessed 15th May, 2020).

www.dfe.gov.uk/schoolsbytype (accessed 19th May, 2020).

www.dfe/academysuccess.org.uk (accessed 20th May, 2020).

Achieving teaching and curriculum excellence

Policy initiatives across the globe have focused on education as the means of improving life chances whilst supporting the ambition for economic prosperity and global stability. Major reform across jurisdictions has become commonplace with world economies borrowing ideas from one another. This has led to rigorous testing regimes as the UK mirrors Chinese systems while China is interested in Western teaching methodologies to encourage creative thinking and innovation in their learners. Drawing on a project that engaged with 11 failing primary schools, this chapter provides evidence that demonstrates the levels of challenge and the expectations for change that pervade modern schooling. As a solution to the drive for excellence the work of McGongill and Doeffer (2017) with nine clearly articulated steps to change is explored. The gradual, clearly articulated and well-planned processes used by effective leaders give clear example to the model of atomic leadership as advocated in this book.

The dominance of Asian communities in international league tables, such as those produced by the Program for International Student Assessment (PISA), has created a discourse which associates the regular use of tests to the pursuit of educational excellence. PISA measures 15-year-old students' reading, mathematics and science literacy and includes measures of general or cross-curricular competencies, such as problem-solving and functional skills acquisition. Despite its distribution to less than 3% of the 35 million 15 year-olds globally, PISA has become the world's premier yardstick for evaluating the quality, equity and efficiency of school systems based mainly on the ability of a sample of learners. PISA data have been awarded high status as a measure of national educational success with cross-national comparisons dominating the concerns of policy analysts. In a globally competitive marketplace educational success is now measured outside national boundaries with achievement levels compared across nations and measured against international standards, (Loveless, 2014).

For many jurisdictions, and certainly in the UK, the publication of PISA data has resulted in a policy discourse from the English government on failing schools, deficit curricula and ineffective teachers. This in turn has led to a redefining of the national curriculum framework for pupils educated in England (Browne and Wong, 2016) with data accepted as the world's premier yardstick for judging a country's education policy, practice and outcomes (Loveless, 2014).

The latest PISA test results published in 2018 show the top three economies or countries for academic achievement to be Shanghai–China, Singapore and Hong Kong–China (OECD, 2018). This international league table, produced by the testing authority, the Organisation for Economic Cooperation and Development (OECD), revealed the United Kingdom (UK) to have improved its ranking up from 22nd to 14th in literacy, in science up to 14th from 15th, and in maths up to 18th from 27th. The data have to be seen in the light of previous periods leading up to the 21st century when Asian countries aspired to Western economic achievements in the aim to 'surpass Britain, catch up with the US'(超英赶美) (Shing, 2014). PISA data are not without their critics. Storey (2004) maintains the data have gained a privileged status among policy-makers and afforded an inappropriate form of authoritative knowledge. Loveless (2014) cautions that the way schools are sampled in a country/economy may affect the test results. Further, Slater (2011) maintains that PISA data are compiled using assumptions which are statistically flawed. Despite this the impact of PISA on UK education policy has been immense as demonstrated by a cadre of government-funded research projects, policy iterations and the reformed content of the national curriculum for all educational stages and phases implemented during the latter part of the last decade (Leithwood et al. 2006; Pont et al. 2008; Cruickshank, 2017; DfE, 2011).

Borrowing ideas from 'successful' nations has become the mantra from the government. This has been particularly prevalent in the area of maths education where the 'Shanghai method' has been advocated and supported by teacher visits to Shanghai in an attempt to model Chinese methods. Resultant from this initiative has been the development of 'maths hubs' across England designed to support the teaching of maths (see Chapter 8).

The use of widespread testing in the English system, first introduced in the late 1980s, has been expanded with tests now for five-year olds in the first few months of their schooling experience. The testing of students at key stages in their academic career has almost become the 'norm' for our learners and the public availability of data to measure school success accepted as common practice (Browne and Wong, 2016). At the close of Chapter 4 a critique was offered of the use of data. This was to offer balance to what had been a positive discussion of the way data is used to prompt collaborative school-to-school support and drive the school improvement agenda. The project described in the following was created as a result of poor results in the national tests and national publicity around 'failing' schools.

The Oxford project

It is difficult to imagine that in an affluent area of the United Kingdom as well-known as Oxford, with its ancient buildings and extensive history, nearly all of the state-funded city schools were experiencing difficulty. This was the case some years ago when the Leadership for Learning (LfL) initiative was launched which involved the two local universities working with leadership teams in 11 primary schools to try and improve learner outcomes.

The selected schools had been identified as falling below 'floor levels' as per the DfE (2011) definition with fewer than 60% of children at age 11 achieving Level 4 or above in the national tests for reading, writing and maths. Table 6.1 shows the combined English and maths assessment data at Key Stage 2, as a percentage of pupils in the cohort, illustrating that some of the schools had been operating 'below the floor' for several years with three having just moved into that category. Schools C and D were defined as 'below the floor' for the four years leading up to the intervention.

 ## The intervention

To address the problem of underachievement in the 11 schools, a change programme was implemented and consisted of three interventions. The first, which for anonymity we will call 'M', involved the purchase of a private company training scheme to support learner achievement in literacy, reading and writing; the second involved the purchase of a numeracy training course from the same company (M); and the third

Table 6.1 School data

	Year 1 English and maths assessment scores at Key Stage 2	Year 2 English and maths assessment scores at Key Stage 2	Year 3 English and maths assessment scores at Key Stage 2	Year 4 English and maths assessment scores at Key Stage 2	Average over four years	Number of times below floor
School A	47	39	37	65	47.00	3
School B	54	44	38	43	47.00	3
School C	49	43	43	58	48.25	4
School D	58	58	51	36	50.75	4
School E	40	40	62	68	52.50	2
School F	49	61	-	48	52.67	2
School G	55	44	53	74	56.50	3
School H	67	59	44	63	58.25	2
School I	66	63	54	62	61.25	1
School J	72	67	61	58	64.50	1
School K	58	69	69	65	65.25	1

involved a programme of continuing professional development (CPD) delivered as a collaborative partnership of educationalists from the two local universities. The third intervention, the so-named Leadership for Learning (LfL) programme comprised a two-year programme with after-school seminars held once a month, monthly training days at a local hotel to which high-profile education leadership specialists were invited and membership of a coaching group or action learning set with regular meetings to share ideas. The intentions implicit in the programme design of the LfL project were to give senior and middle leaders the time and permission to seek and implement new solutions based on research evidence, to provide networks of support to share challenges and to build the confidence of participants in their professional identity and purpose. With these aims achieved it was intended that improvements in pupil outcomes would naturally follow. This approach finds support in the work of Qvortrup (2016) who argues that data- and research-informed professional knowledge increases the professional capital of teachers and school leaders at the individual, social and decisional levels. This he refers to as the 'output effect' of CPD and further maintains that better understanding of performance data and research-informed professional training can have an impact on student learning, achievement and wellbeing. This he maintains improves the reputation of the school, stabilises the pupil population and ultimately enhances the experience of all associated with the school leading eventually to improved teacher retention. The ambition of the LfL project was to create the 'output effect' described by Qvortrup (2016).

To this end the specific objectives of the programme were to:

- Engage the leaders of the city's primary schools in a process of needs identification focused on their schools and their staff.
- Help the leaders to use and share data to analyse and define the challenges that must be addressed in improving attainment of pupils in these schools specifically in reading, writing and maths.
- Engage these leaders with the most robust research and practice, both nationally and internationally.
- Raise attainment by enabling heads to be more effective in leading improvements in teaching and learning.
- Engage teachers in a training programme that directly impacted on teaching methods, the outcome of which should be efforts which were to be reflected in improvements in assessment data.

At the start of the intervention 'a yawning gap' in attainment had been reported for children attending the regions' schools, with performance 'the worst in England at Key Stage 1' (Times Newspaper).

In Chapter 5 of this book the issue of reliance on data, which dominates leadership activity today, was highlighted. The trend towards 'performative' in the governance of education systems, through which layers of external and internal accountability frameworks intrude into all aspects of teachers' work, is not new (Ball, 2003; Troman et al., 2007; Cherubini, 2009; Wilkins, 2015). Proponents argue that this trend, which has come to characterise the global 'modernisation' agenda in education, has contributed to a greater self-confidence, setting in place the essential conditions for a 'self-improving' culture (Hargreaves, 2012:8). Those opposed to the performative system (Galton and MacBeath, 2008; Priestley et al., 2012) argue that schools have become a place where 'commitment, judgement and authenticity within practice are sacrificed for impression and performance' (Priestley et al., 2012:15).

Sachs (2003) argues that leadership dominated by concerns over performance is not an inevitable consequence of the testing regime, that teachers can retain an authentic professionalism and moral purpose by means of a collegial 'activist agency', while others note a possible generational effect, in which younger teachers, the 'products' themselves of increasingly performative schooling, are sanguine about accountability demands, effectively leading to performativity as a normative condition (Evans, 2011; Wilkins, 2015). In this context, a culture in which accountability mechanisms dominate the agenda becomes seen as a 'new common-sense' (Mortimore, 2013:193).

For leaders and aspiring leaders, the performativity issue offers opportunities and challenges. One headteacher, interviewed as part of the LfL project, stated:

> The whole culture around attainment and interpretation of the data has changed. We come together as a whole staff team and look at the data, we don't apply a blame culture and focus on specific staff (well certainly not in our team meetings), we simply identify where our learners are not making the expected progress and then we target those learners for additional support. We have open conversations and agree together where extra support is required (Headteacher, School E).
>
> (McGregor and Browne, 2015)

Other headteachers, when interviewed, described how they had restructured the school; one head described a school where everyone has some responsibility for leadership:

> We want our teachers to have a positive experience of leadership, so they'll take on greater [responsibility and] have a voice. We organised all teachers into leadership teams. Everybody's experiencing leadership. We allow the teams to prioritise their work, set their own challenges and their objectives and we do that in a hands-off way and we budget time money for teachers to do that work. Then, as the head, I talk to each leadership team and ask them to talk through the performance of the team in respect of achieving the targets we have set (Headteacher, School C).
>
> (McGregor and Browne, 2015)

The model of leadership adopted here mirrors that of distributed leadership where responsibilities for leadership are distributed across the school (see Chapter 4 for a more detailed description).

Managing change

It is worth noting some of the external changes that were introduced during the life-time of the project:

- A new OfSTED Inspection Framework was applied using different assessment categories with a hardening of decisions. The third classification of 'satisfactory' was replaced with a 'requires improvement' category.
- A changed focus in OfSTED Inspections which looked specifically at levels of attainment of pupils, their rates of progress and achievement.
- Additional focus on leadership and management.
- A workforce reform agenda with performance measures and career pro-gress linked to annual monitoring of staff achievements against learner performance.
- A new national curriculum was introduced heralding a change in every aspect of what had been taught before, giving teachers a little more freedom within set parameters, but also offering greater responsibility.
- Legislation introduced in 2014 in the form of the Children and Family Act resulted in changes to the funding and arrangements for children with severe special needs. With this came expectation that the role of the Special Educational Needs Coordinator (SENCO) should be one of leadership, leading to changes in the leadership structure in some schools (DfE, 2014).
- Changes to the way teachers assess learning with moves from assessment for learning to assessment without levels (see more on this later in this chapter).
- A major reclassification of some schools required by government to take on academy status (see Chapter 5 for an explanation of the academy movement in English schools).

The last point Table 6.2 illustrates the changing status of the 11 schools involved in the project over a two-year period.

This presents yet another challenge for teachers and their leaders to cope with whilst also trying to improve outcomes for their learners and gain the required grade 2 or 'Good' inspection rating. Such a rating not only shows confidence in the leader-ship team, it means that further visits from the inspectorate are unlikely for some time, unless of course the school data test results show concern.

 ## Leading change through models of collaboration

Setting the scene for leadership in challenging circumstances by describing the Oxford project and identifying the range of policy changes bombarding the leadership teams

Table 6.2 Status change

City schools involved (at varied levels) in the attainment project	At the start of the project	Nearing the end of the project
School A	LA Primary School	**Part of an academy trust**
School B	Voluntary Controlled C of E Primary School	Voluntary Controlled C of E Primary School
School C	LA Primary School	**Part of an academy trust**
School D	LA Primary School	LA Primary School
School E	LA Primary School	LA Primary School
School F	LA Primary School	**Part of an academy trust**
School G	LA Primary School	**Part of an academy trust**
School H	LA Primary School	LA Primary School
School I	C of E Primary School	C of E Primary School
School J	Catholic Primary School	Catholic Primary School
School K	LA Primary School	**Part of an academy trust**

at the time of LfL project offers some insight into the practical challenges of leadership in times of change.

Following extensive research over an eight-year period, McGonagill and Doefffer (2017) describe the nine pillars or steps that needed by those leaders who achieve sustained change, acting as 'architects' who acknowledge the long-term impact of their achievements in building a school organisation that continues to improve year on year.

McGonagill and Doefffer (2017) found that architects sustainably transformed their school by challenging how it operated, engaging its community and improving its teaching. These steps – or atomic changes – were taken over three years following the order set out here.

Step 1: This involved the development of a ten-year plan, clearly showing how the leaders would transform the school and the community it served. The aim was to demonstrate personal commitment and clarify the tough decisions that were ahead.

Step 2: Teach everyone: Expel less than 3% of students. It is vital to make it clear that you are committed to the community and you won't 'off roll' children just to improve test scores. Show parents and teachers that you want to help them. Create support inside the school to manage behaviour and improve internal actions.

Step 3: Teach the children for longer, from ages 5 to 18. Of all the changes made by the leaders in the study, teaching kids for longer was the one with the most consistent impact. It took five years to see results, but test scores improved by nine percentage points and continued to improve by five percentage points each year after that.

Step 4: Challenge the staff: Be prepared to make changes. Focus on exploring how the school works even if it means changing staff. You are there for the students, not the staff, and by protecting one incompetent teacher you are failing the students. One participant reported that with new staff: 'The culture in the school suddenly tipped when we had 30% new staff, people who were serious about trying to transform the school and the community it serves'.

Step 5: Engage students: Keep 95% in class. Focusing on attendance rates with communities of families who don't see the point of education is difficult. Heads in the research claimed it took two years to make students believe in themselves and improve their attendance. This involved inviting external speakers to talk to students to raise aspirations, asking students to evaluate their teachers and join school committees as well acting as mentors to younger students.

Step 6: Challenge the board: Ensure your governors understand that the challenge ahead will take time and don't offer them promises of data improvement that you cannot immediately deliver. Architect leaders are able to emphasise other metrics, such as more students attending classes, more parents coming to parents' evenings and fewer staff member absences. These are data that eventually will lead to the improved test scores the governing body are looking for.

Step 7: Engage parents: Have 50% at parents' evenings. It is important to have the support of your parents right from the start, although it may take time. McGonagill and Doefffer (2017) maintain that this is particularly true in rural or coastal schools in the UK, where people are less mobile and parents and grandparents may have attended the same school. As one architect explained, 'Our parents and grandparents had very strong views about the school based on what it did for them. It took a long time to change these views. But, if we hadn't, then all our hard work would have disappeared when our students went home'.

Attendance at parents' night was as low as 10% when many leaders first arrived – but the most successful ones increased it to more than 50% by the end of the third year. They did this by making it a social event with food, drink and student performances, offering education and support services such as IT skills and career advice, and providing similar services at home through outreach programs.

Step 8: Engage staff: 70% with no absence. Getting staff to support you is another challenge especially where the staff have just been part of a failed inspection and the previous head has left as a result. The environment will be stressful and the new head has to convince the staff that you are there to help and that your presence will make a difference.

One architect described trying to convince a staff, 14 of whom had been on long-term sick leave and only 20% of whom had not been on sick leave, that their jobs would get easier and become more fulfilling if they were prepared to work with her, rather than against her.

Step 9: Ensure you have 100% capable staff. The real problem revealed by McGonagill and Doefffer was recruiting and keeping good staff. Good staff want to work in good schools. The approach taken here by successful heads was to ask local successful schools who had just appointed new staff if they had any recommendations. The most successful schools in the study all had 100% capable staff by the end of the third year. They achieved this by recruiting capable teachers, increasing informal teaching observations (through mentoring programs within and across subjects) and sharing best practices within and across schools. As another architect identified in the research said, 'Too many poor teachers are simply moved from one school to another. We need to develop them, rather than simply passing them on to someone else'.

A further lesson from the research was to 'take time'. School leaders, it argues, are often under huge pressure to turn the school around quickly, but sustainable transformation takes time. In the study, the schools that improved the most in the long term didn't see test score improvements until year three, and continued to get better through year five and beyond. This needs to be explained to the governing body. Change takes time and small atomic steps will have a significant and sustainable impact long after you, the head, have moved on to your next challenge.

The work of McGonagill and Doeffer serves a number of purposes, firstly to demonstrate how effective change can be enacted but secondly to demonstrate atomic leadership in action. The need for small staged steps, taken as part of a comprehensive overarching and clearly articulated plan, is paramount if change is to be sustained over time and have a lasting impact on our schools and learners.

Task 6.1 Critique of the nine steps

Taking the nine steps set out earlier based on the work of McGonagill and Doefffer (2017) assess the processes used in terms of their usefulness for your situation.

In summary, this chapter has addressed the challenges facing leaders today in adapting to changing curricula and meeting expectations for learner excellence.

The competence criteria from the National Professional Qualification for Leadership addressed in this chapter include:

Evaluate the impact of professional development on teacher development and pupil outcomes.

Grow excellent, evidence-based teaching in a team and a curriculum that develops pupils academically and prepares them for adult life.

References

Ball, S.J. (2003) The teacher's soul and the terrors of performativity. *Journal of Education Policy*, 18 (2), 215–228.

Browne, L. and Wong, K.-S. R. (2016) Transnational comparisons of teacher expectation of mathematical functional ability in early years and Key Stage 1 pupils : a study undertaken in Hong Kong and England. *Education 3-13: International Journal of Primary, Elementary and Early Years Education*, 45 (4), 504–515.

Cherubini, L. (2009) Reconciling the tensions of new teachers' socialisation into school culture: a review of the research. *Issues in Educational Research,* 19 (2), 83–99.

Cruickshank, V. (2017) The influence of school leadership on student outcomes. *Open Journal of Social Sciences* 5(9), 115–123. https://www.researchgate.net/journal/2327-5952_Open_Journal_of_Social_Sciences.

Department for Education. (2014) *The children and families act*. Norfolk: Her Majesties Stationery Office.

Department for Education (2011) *School standards*. London: Her Majesties Stationery Office.

Evans, L. (2011) The 'shape' of teacher professionalism in England: professional standards, performance management, professional development and the changes proposed in the 2010 White Paper. *British Educational Research Journal*, 37 (5), 851–870.

Galton, M. and MacBeath, J. (2008) *Teachers under pressure*. London: SAGE.

Hargreaves, D.H. (2012) *A self-improving school system in international context*. Nottingham: National College for School Leadership.

Leithwood, K., Day, C., Sammons, P., Harris, A. and Hopkins, D. (2006) *Seven strong claims about successful school leadership*. Nottingham, National College for School Leadership.

Loveless, T. (2014) The brooking review of PISA. www.brooking.org.uk/pisa' children (accessed 14th September, 2020).

McGongill, M. and Doeffer, R. (2017) *How to create adaptive leaders*. San Francisco, CA: World Institute for Action Learning.

McGregor, D. and Browne, E. (2015) *Report for Oxford City Council*. 14.2.2015.

Mortimore, P. (2013) *Education under siege*. Bristol: Policy Press.

OECD. (2018) Synergies for better learning: an international perspective on evaluation & assessment. [online] Available from: http://www.oecd.org/edu/school/Evaluation_and_ Assessment_Synthesis_Report.pdf [Accessed July 2013]

Pont, B., Nusche, D., and Hunter, M. (2008) School leadership matters. *Improving School Leadership*, Volume 1 Policy and Practice, OECD, 15–39.

Priestley, M., Biesta, G.J.J. and Robinson, S. (2012) *Teachers as agents of change: an exploration of the concept of teacher agency*. Stirling: University of Stirling Press.

Qvortrup, L. (2016) Capacity building: data- and research-informed development of schools and teaching practices in Denmark and Norway. *European Journal of Education for Teachers*, 16 (3), 564–576.

Sachs, J. (2003) *The activist professional.* Buckingham: Open University Press.

Slater, C.L. (2011) Understanding principal leadership: an international perspective and a narrative approach. *Educational Management Administration & Leadership*, 39 (2), 219–227.

Storey, J. (2004) Changing theories of leadership and leadership development. In J. Storey (ed.) *Leadership in organizations: current issues and key trends.* London: Routledge, pp. 11–38.

Times Newspaper. (2016) Schools making exceptional progress. http://www.times.co.uk/education/12896110.xxxxxxx_Primary_School_wins praise_after_making_big_improvement (accessed 20/12/16).

Troman, G., Jeffrey, B. and Raggi, A. (2007) Creativity and performativity policies in primary school culture. *Journal of Education Policy*, 22 (5), 549–572.

Wilkins, C. (2015) Education reform in England: quality and equity in the performative school. *International Journal of Inclusive Education*, 19 (11), 1143–1160.

Wong Kwok Shing, R. (2014) Unpublished keynote presentation at a transnational conference, Edge Hill University, 30th March, 2014.

PART III
Leadership in context

Influencing student learning

Education thinkers around the world give credence to the importance of improving learning opportunities to enable learners to adjust to the complex world we now inhabit whilst policy initiatives give thrust to the purpose of education as improving life chances in this changing world. This chapter explores the influence of leadership on student learning whilst acknowledging that leadership is the conduit by which change is introduced. Such changes might be aimed at improving organisational structures or increasing the positive impact of teaching and learning; they may be initiatives intended for widespread implementation such as innovative approaches to instruction, cooperative learning and changed teacher practice. The focus here is learner-centred leadership and this is explored for the role it can play in supporting schools operating in challenging circumstances.

Good leaders make sense of and productively respond to both external policy initiatives and local needs and priorities. Good leadership practice provides a critical bridge between educational reform initiatives and societal change; it works within contexts to create change within the boundaries that each situation demands. For Yukl, leadership influences

> the interpretation of events for followers, the choice of objectives for the group or organi-
> sation, the organisation of work activities to accomplish objectives, the motivation of
> followers to achieve the objectives, the maintenance of cooperative relationships and
> teamwork and the enlistment of support and cooperation from people outside the group
> to organisation.
>
> (Yuki, 1994:3)

This expansive definition of leadership frames leadership as an active process shaped by context and focused on people. The theoretical model that underpins Yuki's definition might be described within the frame of transformational leadership where leadership practice embraces purpose, people, structures and social systems (Hallinger and Heck, 1996), whilst also setting direction, developing people and designing organisations (Waters, Mazano and McNulty, 2003). In recent times there has been a focus on what has been called learner-centred leadership where leaders strive to create 'learner-centred organisations' and 'professional learning communities' to meet school objectives (Stoll, 2011). Leaders can have a direct and indirect impact on learner outcomes in a variety of ways. These might be the provision of training for teachers, the school's articulated values and culture, the leader's openness in discussing organisational strengths and weaknesses, and the focus on data. These structural approaches can be enhanced by more directed approaches which will be identified shortly. At the structural level learning-centred leadership is

> the simultaneous use of specified strategies in ways which mutually reinforce one another. It is this reinforcement which creates powerful learning for teachers and leaders and which, in turn, informs teachers' actions in classrooms leading to improved teaching and student learning.
>
> (Southworth, 2009:101)

To establish a focus on learning headteachers/leaders might:

* Frequently visit classrooms and participate in professional learning activities with staff.
* Keep up with research and share their learning with others.
* Initiate and guide conversations about student learning.
* Make student learning a focus for school-wide staff meetings.
* Analyse data on student learning and use this for planning to set goals for learning improvement and progress review.

The final point here on data is an interesting one with educational reform initiatives in the US and UK now centred on using achievement tests as a measurement of success, with teachers, leadership and organisations held accountable for their performance. Any discussion of educational leadership must acknowledge the primacy given to data as the key evidence source for leadership effectiveness whilst also acknowledging the need for leaders to be able to articulate the more affective side of the educational endeavour. It is vital that the education endeavour is not taken hostage by an obsession with data and that leaders hold on to the core purpose of education which is to instil in learners a love for learning.

The role of the leader in times of challenge, as described in this text, is that of sense-maker in a climate that is often resistant to change: 'The achievement of change is often dependent upon school culture, collegial support, available resources including time and leadership' (Murphy and Hallinger, 1988:15).

Research in Canada and the US has shown the following approaches to have the most impact for positive change:

1. Learner-focused leadership.
2. Emphasis on student achievement and improvement.
3. Enforcement of government goals.
4. Advocacy and support for specific instructional strategies and a willingness to rethink these if they don't appear to be working.
5. Focus on curriculum knowledge and good interpersonal skills.
6. Systemic monitoring of goals, expectations and standards through effective accountability processes.
7. Direct personal involvement with school practice.
8. Alignment of professional development with school and governmental goals.
9. Systematic use of student testing alongside interrogation of additional data.
10. Goal setting.
11. Tracking school performance.
12. Positive relationships.

(Adapted from Leithwood et al., 2011)

It is important to note that for improvements in pupil achievement to occur educationalists need to hold positive beliefs, expect improvements and have the vision to see what needs to be done and how it might be achieved.

Successful leaders of change believe that all students have the potential for learning that is not fully exploited. Students who enhance their learning capability access their potential by increasing their range of learning skills. This potential is best realised and learning capability enhanced through the range of teaching and learning models that the teacher uses with their students. The deliberate use of a range of teaching and learning strategies with high meta-cognitive content is one of the richest features of learning. The work of Elmore (2004) is useful for giving clarity to any educational approach aimed at making significant improvements to student learning.

Elmore's principles for large scale improvement (in summary) are:

* Create a strong normative environment in which adults take responsibility for the academic performance of children.
* Rely more heavily on face-to-face relationships than on bureaucratic routines.
* Make direct observation of practice, analysis and feedback a routine feature of work. Maintain a tight instructional focus sustained over time.
* Apply the instructional focus to everyone in the organisation.
* Apply it to both practice and performance.

- Apply it to a limited number of instructional areas and practices, becoming pro-gressively more ambitious over time. Routinise accountability for practice and performance in face-to-face relationships.
- Centre group discussions on the instructional work of the organisation.

These clearly delineated stages could well give structure to any improvement plan designed by an aspiring headteacher. The stages follow the criteria of modelling, monitoring and encouraging open dialogue identified in the following as part of a learner-centred leadership approach.

Learner centred leadership in context

Learner-centred leadership, as implied earlier, incorporates a range of strategies such as modelling, monitoring, and open approaches to dialogue (Southworth, 2004, 2009, 2011) alongside approaches such as mentoring and coaching (West-Burnham and Coates, 2005) with instructional leaders striving to create 'learner-centre organization[s]' and 'professional learning communities' to meet school objectives. As seen in Chapter 4 school systems and structures can facilitate a learner-centred approach and impact the whole school and other organisations where a strong leader might be offering support. School leaders, whether they be National Leaders of Learning, headteachers in effective schools or middle leaders, can influence what goes on in the classroom indirectly through the use of the strategies identified ear-lier. Coaching, and the creation of action learning sets which bring leaders together to discuss their challenges in a protected environment, has proved to be extremely effective in a number of school and further education interventions (Browne, 2013; McGregor and Browne, 2015).

The strategies used by leaders to maintain a persistent focus on the learner include practical things like making time for a leadership team 'learning walk' once a week, where the head and/or the leadership team visit every classroom in the school and talk to the learners. Teaching and learning can become a permanent item on a staff meeting agenda and part of any formal discussion such as those at staff performance reviews, in newsletters home to parents and with school governors. The leadership team may wish to set a good example themselves by pursuing some academic study, by sharing the results of research or by carrying out small-scale research projects in the school. In some cases leadership team members, including the headteacher, still engage in teaching.

The focus on school data and the regular analysis of patterns and trends has been discussed in previous chapters. Learner-centred leadership will interrogate data not explored to challenge performance but presented illustratively as an instrument which informs and guides decision-making. The following case study shows how one school is using data in an informed and effective way to drive improvements.

Case study 7.1 Thomas Reade Primary School

Thomas Reade Primary School is a high-performing school in Oxfordshire, proud of its status as the first OfSTED outstanding school in the town where it is situated. The staff were advised to use a particular maths scheme to boost its results, with some high-achieving pupils having extra online lessons from an expert in Shanghai. Based on 'in class' assessments, it became apparent that some learners were failing to grasp basic concepts as they progressed through the national curriculum requirements. The headteacher, as a Local Leader of Education, observed similar trends in a school he was supporting which was using the same scheme. As a result, the school changed its approach and other schools, supported by the headteacher, were advised to do the same. With a data-informed approach, the results for numeracy for a range of schools in the region were much higher than might have otherwise been. Numeracy became an agenda item on all meetings, staff were asked to note achievements and these were celebrated, and a regular focus was given to numeracy in the school newsletter. In addition, parents were invited into the school for a special event entitled 'How can I Help my Child Learn to Love Maths?' The results for the school in the next set of national tests increased from 61% of children achieving the desired level to 89%.

There are a range of components that facilitate a learning-centred leadership approach that require leaders to be adapt at modelling new approaches and able to plan effectively for productive curriculum delivery, conscious of time, units of work, class sizes and the needs of individual students. A recent move in the English education system has been to give more credence to the role of staff concerned with learners who have special needs. The SENDCO (Special, Education Needs and Disability Coordinator) is now, in many schools, a member of the leadership team in all phases of education. The SENDCO is vital in supporting the leadership team in monitoring performance, setting targets, communicating ideas and vision, analysing data, looking at individual student needs and supporting staff in addressing differentiated learner needs. The SENDCO may influence school policies and work with learning support assistants (or teaching support staff) to ensure learner needs are met. The SENDCO role as part of the leadership team is such that on 21 February 2020 'SENDCOs Make Brilliant Head Teachers' was a headline published in the Times Education Supplement (www.timeseducationsupplement21.2.20).

Learning-centred leadership goes beyond the role of the SENDCO to be central to the operating systems of the whole school with leadership meetings focused on monitoring student progress on a student-by-student basis whilst also offering coaching to colleagues to address issues that become apparent.

For leaders to influence learning the leadership team needs to be involved and exercise influence in a sustained way and at a range of levels:

1. With pupils, encouraging them to think about their abilities and skills as learners.
2. With adults, by working with staff teams, encouraging an open culture, celebrating success and sharing 'what works' with different learners.
3. By leading learning and offering leadership development by coaching and supporting staff.
4. By focusing on school-wide learning so that staff focus on student learning.
5. By working in partnership through a systems approach (see Chapter 4) by working together.
6. As part of a network of schools collaborating, sharing approaches and gaining from a collaborative approach

(Adapted from Southworth, 2009:105–7)

Research carried out in the United States (Shatzer et al., 2014) focused on comparing the effects of learner-centred leadership with the more traditional approach known as transformational leadership. They worked with 590 teachers in 37 elementary schools asking them to rate their principals' leadership style account using specific rating scales. The research identified a number of principal behaviours, central to a learning-focused model of leadership, that appeared to have the greatest impact on student learning. Namely, these were the capability to:

- Meet with teachers to discuss students' needs.
- Discuss performance results with teachers and students.
- Limit possible interruptions to classroom instruction.
- Encourage teachers to use classroom time effectively.
- Recognise students who exhibit academic excellence or improvement.
- Provide clear expectations and appropriate rewards for teachers.
- Provide recognition at assemblies and office visits and in communications to parents.

There is a clear need for school leaders and principals to have their finger on the button of the core operational aspects of the school, to be in touch with educational matters and know the right thing to do, and say the right thing at the right time to the right people, acknowledging those who are aiming high and achieving within as much as they are able.

The research by Shatzer et al. (2014) identifies with the work of Levin (2013) to acknowledge that student background, school context and demographics impact on a leader's ability to lead.

Task 7.1 Assessing challenge

How would you assess 'challenging circumstances'?
How do you avoid deficit thinking when working with colleagues?
How could learner-centred leadership work in your context?

How do we measure challenging circumstances?

The term 'challenging circumstances' is coined to describe schools whose geographic location is in an area of adverse economic conditions, with high unemployment and key elements of social challenge such as extensive and disruptive drug abuse, family breakdown and crime. Low family income and low parental skills and/or training may be an influencing factor specifically where parents have no aspirations or where education is undervalued.

In some cases, the school may experience limited parental involvement with some parents challenging the basic standards and expectations of the school. Pupil attendance rates may be low and well below the national average. In such circumstances teaching posts remain hard to fill and schools operate with high levels of temporary staff. In terms of an available indicator that can be accessed as part of the published data about a particular school, the proportion of free school meals and SEN scores can also offer contextual evidence of some of the challenges present in any particular school.

For headteachers leading schools that are operating in challenging circumstances (see the LfL project in Chapter 6) it is essential to stay positive and avoid a deficit model of education. Easier said, perhaps, than achieved. The deficit model promotes the idea that low achievement in schools is due to problems with the pupils themselves, their families and their communities. This approach fails to see the role of the school, its instructional practices, its organisational structures and its reason for being as being key to pupil attainment.

Learner-centred leadership has been found to be effective in schools operating with high levels of deprivation (Levin, 2013) with effective leadership identified as giving focus to supporting, evaluating and developing teacher quality (Pont et al.,

2008). Supporting teacher performance requires the backing of a leadership team willing to observe teachers in the classroom and offer constructive feedback. Leaders collectively need to coordinate the curriculum and teaching programmes, monitor and evaluate teaching, promote professional development and support collaborative working cultures whilst challenging teachers' assumptions and fostering a learning atmosphere.

Research carried out in the United States has highlighted how effective school leadership can grow the expertise of teachers and increase their confidence and social capital (Minkler, 2014). Minckler identifies the dispositions, knowledge and skills demonstrated by effective school leaders who are able to bridge the gap between mediocrity and achievement by optimising the effectiveness of their teachers. Placing high importance on the relational aspect of leadership, Minckler demonstrates how membership of social networks, which Minckler refers to as social capital, can have a high impact on teacher performance and school outcomes.

Research based on four case studies carried out in schools in Ghana identified how a focus on training headteachers to adopt leadership for learning capabilities had a positive impact on the quality of teaching and learning and on the capacity of heads to revitalise their staff and communities (Malakolunthu et al., 2014).

Task 7.2 Structures of support

Identify examples, within the structural organisation of a school with which you are familiar, that support collaboration and encourage collaborative learning models. Evaluate their effectiveness and design and/or deliver, in collaboration with team members, an activity or meeting that will have collaboration at its heart.

This chapter has introduced the important role played leadership teams in setting positive and ambitious goals for schools and identified the academic literature which gives focus to what is known as 'learner-centred leadership'. This leadership style is considered particularly productive when applied in schools operating in challenging circumstances.

In Chapter 10 more focus is given to the role of CPD in driving the improvement culture in our schools. The English qualification framework is described and evidence gleaned from other countries as to how CPD is managed. The leadership focus in Chapter 10 is underpinned by the theoretical approach known as instructional leadership.

The competences for the National Professional Qualifications for Leadership covered in this chapter are:

Support teams to build and sustain relationships with others which develops and shares good practice and improves performance.
Recognise strengths and weaknesses and identify learning linked to needs.

References

Browne, E. (2013) *Running a business unit in a UK University*. Education Provocations, Auckland University of Technology: Printset AUT, pp. 89–99.

Elmore, R.F. (2004) *School reform from the inside out*. Cambridge, MA: Harvard Education Press.

Hallinger, P. and Heck, R.H. (1996) Reassessing the Principal's role in schools effectiveness: a review of empirical research. *School Effectiveness and School Improvement*, 9 (2), 157–191.

Leithwood, K., Seashore, L.M., Anderson, S. and Wahlstrom, K. (2011) *How leadership influences student learning*. London: Department for Education.

Levin, M. (2013) *Confident school leadership*. Nottingham: NCSL.

Malakolunthu, S., McBeath, J. and Swaffield, S. (2014) Improving the quality of teaching and learning through leadership for learning: changing scenarios in basic schools in Ghana. *Journal of Educational Management, Administration and Leadership*, 42 (5), 701–717.

McGregor, D. and Browne, E. (2015) Report to Oxford City Council – Leadership for learning. Available at www.oxfordcitycouncilcommitteedreport/13.2.15

Minkler, C.H. (2014) School leadership that grows teacher social capital. *Journal of Educational Management, Administration and Leadership*, 42 (5), 657–679.

Murphy, J. and Hallinger, P. (1988) The characteristics of instructionally effective school districts. *Journal of Educational Research*, 81(3), 176–181.

Pont, B., Nusche, D. and Hunter, M. (2008) School leadership matters. In *Improving school leadership: volume 1: policy and practice*, Paris: OECD, pp. 15–39.

OECD (2018) *Education and training policy improving on system leadership*. Paris: OECD Publications.

Schatzer, R., Caldarella, P. and Hallam, P. (2014) Comparing the effects of instructional and transformational leadership on student achievement: implications for practice. *Journal Educational Management Administration and Leadership*, 42 (4), 231–242.

Southworth, G. (2004) Learning-centred leadership. In Davies, B. (ed.) *The essentials of school leadership*. London: SAGE, pp. 45–47.

Southworth, G. (2009) Learning-centred leadership. In Davies, B. (ed.) *The essentials of school leadership*: 2nd ed. London: SAGE, pp. 156–166.

Southworth, G. (2011) Learning-centred leadership. In Davies, B. (ed.) *The essentials of school leadership*: 2nd ed. London: SAGE, pp. 23–45.

Stoll, L. (2011) Leading professional learning communities. In Robinson, J. and Timperley, H. (eds.) *Leadership and learning*. London: Sage, pp. 245–267.

Times Education Supplement. The SENDCO role as part of the leadership team is such that Feb. 21st, 2020. SENDCOs Make Brilliant Head Teachers www.timese ducationsupplement_sencosmakebrilliantheadteachers21.2.20 (accessed 25.2.20).

Waters, T. Mazano, R.J. and McNulty, B. (2003) Balanced leadership: what 30 years of research tells us about the effect of leadership on student achievement. *Aurora MidCounties Research for Education Leadership.* www.mcrel.org

West-Burnham, J. and Coates, M. (2005) *Personalised learning, transforming education for every child.* Stafford: Network Education Press.

Yuki, G. (1994) *Leadership in organisations.* 3rd ed. Englewood Cliffs, NJ: Prentice Hall.

Knowledge mobilisation and followership

As a result of the challenges faced in the VUCA world the role of education in establishing global and local links has become paramount. Without conversation and the opportunity to clarify meaning, so that we can learn from one another, we will not grow. Now, more than ever before, it is important to work collaboratively and share good practice. In advocating an atomic leadership approach this chapter focuses on different examples of excellence observed in schools across the world. The aim is to share good practice, to focus on effective partnerships in operation and offer ideas that might produce small steps that lead to atomic change in our schools.

The focus on excellence

Jurisdictions around the world have been focused on the Sustainable Development Goals set by UNESCO aimed at securing a quality education for all by 2030. By articulating a number of Sustainable Development Goals, world experts have set down in writing ambitions for inclusive and equitable quality education for all. This is driven by the desire to give the next generation the tools to fight poverty and prevent disease. UNICEF working in tandem with UNESCO has called for high-quality, child-friendly basic education for all, focusing on gender equality and the elimination of disparities of all kinds (UNESCO, 2014).

Knowledge leadership

To achieve the Sustainable Development goals for education in times of difficulty, leaders will need to employ a leadership approach known as 'knowledge leadership', defined by Stogdill (1974) as a process whereby an individual supports other group members in learning processes needed to attain group or organisational goals. This definition is relevant today alongside the perspective that leaders need loyal and committed followers, emphasising that leaders do not exist in isolation. In addition, leaders are products of the time and the environment they inhabit, having today to be prime movers working collaboratively with others to achieve common goals (Weller and Weller, 2002). Effective leaders command and also serve their followers. They listen to ideas and make choices whilst also providing direction on how desired ends might be achieved.

Knowledge is a valuable resource and a driver for organisations to make changes. It forms part of the decision-making process and leaders need to be well informed and thoughtful when making decisions. Leaders must consider decisions from multiple perspectives and this can be complex.

In the industrial era knowledge was focused around production and ensuring young learners acquired the knowledge needed to exist in an industrially focused environment. Today, as society is adjusting to major international upheaval, new types of leadership, based on knowledge around learner achievement, improvement targets and organisational effectiveness, have become the mantra.

For leaders the important thing is to make well-informed decisions as the application of data analytics and big data, along with artificial intelligence and fake news, impact on a leader's ability to make decisions. Making decisions has never been more complex and information and 'facts' from multiple sources impinge on the process on a daily basis. Koskinen et al. (2011) describe the issues facing decision-makers as leading to 'wicked problems' only to be analysed and understood through the VUCA environment

The term 'wicked problem' refers to the complex, confusing and multifaceted problems in social systems that are difficult, or even impossible, to solve in a clear-cut manner. The concept was popularised by German design theorist Horts-Rittel (2011) in the mid-1960s.

Examples of these problems abound today. So, for example, how do we combat the impact of climate change, how do we support thousands of refugees from war-torn countries, how do we respond to disease and pandemics that threaten world order?

Wicked problems consist of issues that affect multiple networks and according to Weber and Khademian (2008) we need to build effective networks in our society to establish the capacity for long-term collaborative problem solving. The wicked problems we might encounter might be unstructured, offering limited opportunity for definition and capture; they might be cross-cutting, impacting on all areas of the system, and relentless, such as the demands for improvements in school performance data on an annual basis with schools experiencing the fear of inspection and audit on a daily basis.

The wicked problems faced in a global world highlight the challenge of knowledge management. School leaders have to be able to address complex issues and interpret knowledge from a range of sources. Information is core but effective leaders need to be able to use knowledge with intelligence and be prepared to challenge some of the evidence offered (Browne, 2013).

In the spirit of knowledge sharing this chapter now focuses on a range of projects and innovations from a collection of different schools that are impacting on the learner experience, providing opportunities for the disadvantaged and improving life chances.

Knowledge sharing: The London Challenge

Mention has already been made of the London Challenge as a particularly important programme in London's school improvement process (see Chapter 4). The programme's first phase (2003–8) targeted secondary schools, and the second phase (2008–11) continued to work with secondary schools but also extended the programme's reach to primary schools.

The London Challenge targeted whole districts within London identified as causes for concern, as well as specific underperforming schools – termed 'Keys to Success' (KTS) schools – across the city. The programme involved a range of school improvement initiatives, many of which made use of the expertise of the best practitioners and best schools, with an emphasis on school-to-school knowledge transfer.

Much of the school improvement activity centred on building relationships between high-performing and underperforming schools. This involved the sharing of expertise and training for leaders and teachers in underperforming schools, with the package of support for each school tailored and brokered by a London Challenge adviser. In particular, the programme developed the concept of system leadership by pioneering the use of expert headteachers to mentor the headteachers of underperforming schools. An independent evaluation found that KTS schools improved at a faster rate than the national average using a range of metrics.

Interest in the long-term impact of this initiative led to the commissioning of research, carried out in 2018, which found that the initiative had had long-term impact, to the extent that a 'self-improving' school system had been established and still existed. The report argues that the key resource for school development is the collective expertise within the schools themselves rather than the work of external school improvement agencies. The project, it was concluded, had created internal links and capacity for school-to-school improvement with knowledge shared in a spirit of collegiality which was maintaining and driving school improvement across the city (McAleavy et al. 2019).

Knowledge sharing: Ending pupil referrals – Sport and Thought

A school in Brent, in northwest London, had one of the worst exclusion rates in the country. Prior to the Sport and Though intervention the school was dealing with over 100 episodes of negative behaviour on a weekly basis; now it has two or three pupils removed from the classroom per week and no exclusions and there are minor infringements of school's rules.

The headteacher, Daniel Coyle, writes in the school prospectus: 'Everyone counts, everyone contributes, everyone succeeds' (www.newmanschool.org).

These are bold ambitions in an area where there is high unemployment with large numbers of new immigrant families and numerous learners for whom English is a second language.

'Brent is a north west, Outer London borough. It is generally a poor area, with 33% of households living in poverty, and 31% of employees earning less than the London Living Wage' (https://www.trustforlondon.org.uk/data/boroughs/brent-poverty-and-inequality-indicators).

With great foresight the school leadership team invited a company called 'Sport and Thought' to work with a disaffected and often excluded group of learners. Through football they worked with the learners to operate a PRP approach – pause, reflect, progress – on the football pitch whilst also helping the students to then use this in their classroom interactions. This psychodynamic thinking approach has worked with learners, helping them to block negative thoughts and focus on personal strengths.

OfSTED say of the school:

> Pupils' contexts are often very complex and they require multiple agency support in order to meet their needs and enable them to be active British citizens. Many pupils arrive on a weekly basis, with little or no spoken English, and need significant and intensive support in order to access the curriculum and society as a whole.
>
> (www.newmanschool.ofstedreport)

The report goes on the praise the Sport and Thought intervention with the school now acting as a respite centre for excluded pupils across the borough as challenging matters of discipline do not occur in this school.

The Sport and Thought website states:

Sport and Thought works with school age children with behavioural difficulties who are at high risk of exclusion. Sport and Thought is a way of working with adolescents/children that fuses the sport of football, the symbolism of the sports coach and psychodynamic theory. We create a space to encourage thought and act as a catalyst to promote emotional and behavioural change. Our aim is to help young people develop the emotional control and resilience they need to participate actively in school, complete their education and lead fulfilling, emotionally rich lives. We undertake work on the football pitch and within more traditional educational environments. Within both arenas our theoretical framework remains the same.

In addition to the practical Sport and Thought sessions, we also offer:

- Respite provision for secondary age students in partnership with Newman Catholic College Brent (Pause, Reflect, Progress space)
- Individual mentoring, secondary and primary
- Group mentoring, secondary and primary
- Class-based individual lesson support at both secondary and primary levels (Behaviour coaching)
- Delivery of soft sports-based qualifications
- Training modules in our way of working
- School SLT support
- Football in the psychological context

We believe an individual's reactions within a sporting context are no different to a societal one. If one reacts aggressively to a perceived wrong in the field of play or has difficulty with another player being within their proximity, it is quite likely such a reaction will be mirrored within the classroom and life in general. The sport of football can be used to enable participants to consider their own emotional and behavioural traits, and the underlying reasoning behind them. Sport and Thought works with its membership to slow down their internal processes and anxieties. This allows them to reflect and not consistently act on impulse. By doing this we begin to create a more robust internal state of being.

(www.sportandthought.com)

Sport and Thought are now expanding their work into Milton Keynes and Oxfordshire.

Knowledge sharing: Working in partnership

An example of schools working in partnership can be found in Milton Keynes where a leadership centre has been established, formed on the idea of a 'web and tentacle' model to allow school leadership teams to support one another. Leadership training is offered in a specially allocated building on the campus of one of the partner schools and senior leaders, middle leaders and aspiring leaders organise training and CPD events to support the drive for continuous improvement in their area.

 ## Knowledge mobilisation: Another sporting example

Another London-centric activity is the work of the Newlands Academy in London. Here, headteacher Gareth Howells encourages disadvantaged and disengaged learners to experience the Ebony Horse Club. One of the few remaining horse training venues in London, Ebony works with students who might otherwise be excluded from school to encourage strong communication, work ethic and friendship-building with animals and people. The project is working particularly well with students with learning difficulties who sometimes find it easier to communicate with animals than people (www.newlandsacademy.org).

 ## Knowledge mobilisation: Research into the use of pupil premium

Within the English education system pupils defined as 'disadvantaged' warrant an additional payment from the government known as the 'pupil premium'. This is a payment to the school per designated pupil, designed to be used to help disadvantaged children make progress in line with their more advantageous peers.

Whilst schools can gain the pupil premium grant for children in a variety of disadvantaged contexts, the main reason a child will gain this is because they are in receipt of free school meals due to low household income. Data from national tests show that, as expected, disadvantaged pupils are significantly underperforming academically compared to their more advantaged peers. The pupil premium grant funds schools to deliver additional provision to reduce the attainment gap and improve disadvantaged students' future prospects. Research carried out by Raine (2019) illustrated the various approaches taken by school leaders in the use of pupil premium funding. Her research revealed that the funding did not always reach the pupils for whom it was intended, being spent more generally as a 'top up fund' for out-of-school activities, or in schools where there is financial hardship, as a fund for basic operational requirements. The research concluded that getting parents to support their children and encouraging closer operational links between the family and the child's school might be the best way forward.

Knowledge mobilisation: Partnership working between the independent and state sectors.

Abingdon School in Oxfordshire, a fee-paying independent school, has recently funded the purchase of a new state-of-the-art science block. Funding was enhanced by donations from alumni and local scientists. The block contains a model of the Haldon Collider Scope, donated by a parent who is a highly regarded international scientist. A model of collegiate partnership has been operating between this independent school and one of the local state schools. Sixth form pupils from the independent school have been working 1–1 with pupils from the state school, the teachers from the state school have been given access to the state-of-the-art science rooms for A level teaching sessions and some partnership teaching in the state school has worked well for the staff in Abingdon School who have been able to observe teaching strategies used by trained experts in the state sector designed to motivate the less engaged learner.

Knowledge mobilisation: Learning from the private sector

Research by Bailey and Gibson (2019) has shown that where a school has been taken over and rebranded as an academy the important element of success was to change the 'our kids can't do that' culture to a 'can do' culture. Where, for example, independent and established schools with long-standing traditions have taken over failing schools (Wellington School in Somerset) and introduced a house system, as well as other elements considered part of the independent school culture such as interhouse team events, sports challenges, prefects and house captains, the reports are very positive (Bailey and Gibson, 2019).

Knowledge mobilisation: Maths hubs

In the spirit of sharing expert knowledge, the English government funded the establishment of a number of regional maths hubs where teachers and leaders can share good practice around the teaching of maths. Appreciation for the benefits of these hubs is clearly articulated in the words of Jamie Davies, head of Sydney Russell School in East London: 'The only way we can keep teachers fresh, alive and high quality is to allow teachers headroom. It is time spent working with colleagues in the Maths Hubs' (www.sydneyrussell.org.uk).

Knowledge mobilisation: Support for the sixth form student

One school in London Borough of Southwark – which has a high proportion of disadvantaged pupils – opens at 6:30 am every school day so that sixth formers can do work.

Another school, in North London, has the names of universities on the classroom doors to break down barriers – Oxford University is on the lips of every pupil, even if they initially don't understand where it is and have no ambition to attend it.

Wellington Private School, a sponsored state school academy, introduced the house system and formal uniforms to create culture of pride in their school.

Knowledge mobilisation: The use of meetings, an international view

Research carried out in India has focused on time spent in meetings. Entitled 'Unplanned Meeting: The hidden gem in educational leadership' (Midha, 2020), the research uses the lens of 'principal meetings' to observe different types of interactions lead educationalists engage in and how these meetings shape thought and action. What Midha discovered is that more impactful conversations occur in the corridor than in a formal meeting. Such meetings occur on the way to the principal's office, in a hallway or when a teacher just 'pops in' to the office without a prearranged meeting time.

The research produced three interconnecting themes:

- Unplanned meetings compromise a large portion of a principal's time. Such meetings tend to be short and can involve the principal in quick decision-making and speedy responses within a short time when compared to formally planned meetings.
- Planned and unplanned meetings serve different purposes. The research revealed that planned meetings are essential for disseminating information from government and other agencies and for recording actions in case of inspection or litigation claims. They are usually focused on what needs to be done in a given time

scale and act as the engine that drives action in the institution. In summary, they are task-setting.

- Unplanned meetings tend to be about clarification. Teachers will ask specific questions about how to achieve tasks. Midha found it to be common for a teacher to ask specific questions such as 'Can you tell me how to complete the new classroom observation checklist?'

So, what can we take from this research? Consider the following task.

Task 8.1 Evaluate the time spent in meetings

It is suggested that in the spirit of atomic leadership, and in whatever leadership role you inhabit, that you keep a diary for one week.

First, record briefly how much time you spend in formal meetings and what these meetings achieve in terms of actions and outcomes.

Second, record how many informal work-related conversations you take part in, whether these be in the corridor, the staff room, the car park, etc. The sort of 'can I just catch you for a minute?' questions.

Record the theme of these questions and whether the discussion was functional, having a purpose to support the key ambitions of the school. Note also the time spent answering them.

At the end of the week compare the two lists and calculate the time spent on each.

These two lists should enable you to make some reasonably sound assumptions based on the following questions:

Do formal meetings achieve what is intended?
Is enough time or too much time spent in formal meetings?

Do staff ask unnecessary questions of the leadership team, and if so why is this the case? Is there a problem with communication in the school? Are staff from one team seemingly more needy than others? Is there a problem with the team leader?

You may wish to explore a range of other questions that spring from the data you have collected.

Finally, does the school have the right balance between formal meetings and informal conversations? Are you accessible enough? Would the school work better if you spent more time in the corridors on informal meetings and less time in your office?

Knowledge mobilisation: Creativity

In a 2015 World Economic Forum report the top four competencies required for students to approach complex challenges were found to be critical thinking, creativity, communication and collaboration. The importance of creativity and creative thinking has also been emphasised by global business bodies like UNESCO; international educational bodies like PISA; and the OECD. In the UK, the CBI has recognised the importance of creativity to our economic future as has the All-Party Design and Innovation Group. According to the Economic Graph (a digital representation of the global economy based on 590 million LinkedIn members, 50 thousand skills, 30 million companies, 20 million open jobs and 84 thousand schools) creativity is the second most desirable competency in an employee (after cloud computing) (OECD, 2015).

A survey conducted by Britain Thinks asked headteachers and school governors their views on creativity in education. An online survey of 396 headteachers and governors was followed up with telephone interviews with 54 of the participants. The survey highlighted tensions between positive attitudes about creativity among participants and how it is actually prioritised in schools. Headteachers thought it important to support creativity and creative thinking. They associated creativity with problem solving, expression and communication. Many thought that, when inculcated effectively, creativity could increase pupils' confidence and resilience and deliver improvements in their attainment grades for core subjects.

The Durham Commission on Creativity and Education identified the need for support from leadership teams if creativity is to be encouraged in schools. Funding was required alongside a culture of communication and freedom of expression. From the Durham research it is apparent that there are issues for headteachers to grapple with especially if aiming to embed creativity across all subjects and all aspects of their schools. Support and reassurance from school leaders is no doubt crucial for any substantial impact to be achieved (Turner et al., 2013).

One school that has been praised for its focus on creativity is Thomas Tallis School in London. 'Tallis Habits' are embedded in every subject of the school using the five-dimensional model of creativity developed by the Centre for Real-World Learning at the University of Winchester, following a decade of empirical research by Lucas and Spencer (2017). The Tallis model makes clear to staff and students the key words associated with each creative habit, the kinds of opportunities which they expect all students to experience and suggested pedagogies for staff to use in their teaching. Students are encouraged to use a Tallis Habits Journal to record the development of their creativity.

To establish this philosophy of global engagement the school has designed an agreement which is signed by parents/careers, children and all staff at the school. It is written as a form of contract wilt obligations and expectations on all parties.

The Tallis Agreement

The school will:
- Treat all members of the school with respect and understanding.
- Give regular feedback on progress through marking, reports and the planner.
- Provide full access to the school's facilities and resources.
- Set work which is appropriate to age and ability.
- Set regular and appropriate homework.
- Provide a high standard of teaching.
- Provide secure, well-organised and appropriate learning environments.
- Provide good pastoral support through a tutor and Pastoral Leader.
- Contact parents/carers if there is a problem with attendance, punctuality, uniform or equipment.
- Let parents/carers know about persistent problems that affect their child's work.
- Arrange Parents Evenings, timed according to the needs of the year group involved, at which your child's progress will be discussed.
- Have the right to withdraw a student from the mainstream curriculum or exclude a student from school for breaches of discipline.
- Keep parents/carers informed about school activities through regular letters home, newsletters and notices about special events

Thomas Tallis School, Kidbrooke Park Road, London SE3 9PX

As a Tallis student, I agree to:
- Treat all members of the school with respect and understanding.
- Aim for 100% attendance.
- Arrive at school and in lessons on time.
- Bring my planner, books, equipment and PE kit.
- Work hard in class.
- Complete homework on time.
- Always wear the correct school uniform.
- Look after school property and its environment, keeping it free from litter and graffiti.
- Help maintain the good reputation of the school in the local area.

As parent(s)/carer(s) I/we agree to:
- Treat all members of the school with respect and understanding.
- Ensure my/our child's excellent attendance and punctuality, informing the school promptly about any absence or other concerns.
- Encourage my/our child with work, including daily homework.
- Ensure my/our child has a well-stocked pencil case, a calculator, a dictionary and a strong bag.
- Ensure my/our child wears the correct school uniform and PE kit, clearly marked with his/her name.
- Read, inspect and sign my/our child's planner at least weekly.
- Contribute to the cost of repair or replacement as a result of wilful damage of school property.
- Support the school in its standards and policies including punishments, detailed in the prospectus 'Information for Parents'.
- Arrange family holidays during the scheduled school holidays but where this is impossible, I/we will seek permission from the Headteacher beforehand.
- Attend Parents Evening and discussions about my/our child's progress.

T: +44 (0)208 856 0115   F: +44 (0)208 331 3004   E: headteacher@thomastallis.org.uk

(www.tallisschool.org.uk)

Knowledge sharing: Assessment methods

An approach adopted by Varndean College in Brighton has embraced the idea of a culture of excellence with a number of working groups looking at various pillars of teaching and learning. The school leadership team, along with the staff, have adopted a deliberate strategy aimed at improving the use and understanding of academic language.

There has been an all-encompassing approach across the school, in written work, on school displays, in assemblies and in other interactions on the use of appropriate language. Complex, subject-specific words are applied regularly, in appropriate contexts and with their meanings added. Pupils are challenged on the use of colloquial words in their answers to questions and asked to respond more formally.

The school has found that one of the most powerful ways to drive the desired improvement in language use is through modelling. So, a teacher may pose a question and then answer it whilst explaining their thought process in front of the class. The technique can be adapted so that a piece of work is produced as a class and developed through carefully planned questioning.

Task 8.2 A 'can do' culture

Does your organisation have a 'can do' culture? Do conversations focus on what participants achieve? Are conversations which offer a negative response always challenged?

The challenges of the world we live in, in VUCA times, has been mentioned in Chapter 1. Given the turbulence in the world, our educational institutions should be places of support and stability, with cultures that foster a making-sense approach that helps young people manage their lives with resilience and confidence.

 ## Knowledge mobilisation: Assessment models

In Chapter 7 a range of policy initiatives were identified that have impacted on English schools and school leadership teams. One of these, linked to the introduction of the new national curriculum, related to assessment methodologies.

Schools have been required to align all their assessments to key elements of the curriculum and record pupil achievement against the criteria set out in the national curriculum subject guidelines.

Individual pupil records are expected to show step-by-step progress as children reach or exceed the key stage expectations in the new curriculum. A complex tracking exercise has to be carried out for each child in each key subject area so that teachers and leaders can measure whether pupils are on track to meet key stage expectations. St Aloysius School, the subject of the following case study, states on its website:

> Through rigorous and timely assessment of and feedback to our pupils, St Aloysius will ensure that all pupils achieve their maximum potential. The attainment of each pupil will be measured against the end-of-year Age-Related Expectations and reported as falling within one of four categories:
>
> Emerging – Working below the year group expectations
>
> Developing – Working within the year group expectations but not yet secure in the end of year expectations.
>
> Secure – Pupils have achieved the majority of the end of year expectations (most children will achieve this standard).
>
> Mastery – Fully secure in almost all or all the end of year expectations and is able to use and apply their knowledge and skills confidently.
>
> (www.staloysiusschool.com)

The expectation is that, once a child reaches a level of competence in a subject domain, more depth and breadth are added to their knowledge, with more opportunities available to develop their using and apply skills in a mastery and depth approach.

The purpose of this chapter was to share some of the approaches to school improvement being trialled in schools across the world. As national governments set complex goals for education in the 21st century they are simultaneously devolving more authority to schools for deciding how to meet these goals and holding schools more accountable for results. Simply stated, England deploys its best principals to help schools in need of support. Singapore has a proactive approach to identifying and developing educator talent, recruiting teachers from the top one-third of their cohort and assessing them early on for leadership potential. In Shanghai, the principal's role focuses on the overall performance of the school, but much of the instructional leadership of the school is carried out by teaching and research groups. In Ontario, Canada, the defining feature of the education initiative is its focus on building capacity in schools to raise achievement.

What this chapter has tried to do is share some of the excellent practice that is underway in our schools and to advocate, in line with the atomic leadership model of school leadership, a stepped approach that could potentially have very powerful influences on the children we teach.

The competencies for the National Professional Qualification for Leadership covered in this chapter are:

* Research into, and examples of, interventions targeted at improving the progress/attainment of disadvantaged groups or those with particular needs, drawn from a range of schools
* Research into, and examples of, effective partnership working, drawn from a range of schools,
* Research into, and examples of, structures and processes that support collaboration (for example, with teachers, teaching assistants and non-teaching staff, other schools, parents/carers and other organisations, drawn from a range of schools
* Research into, and examples of, curriculum development approaches/techniques

References

Bailey, L. and Gibson, M. (2019) International school principals: routes to headship and key challenges of their role. *Journal of Educational Management Administration and Leadership*, 47 (3), 1–19.

Browne, E. (2013) *Running a business unit in a UK University*. Education Provocations, Auckland University of Technology. Printset AUT, pp. 89–99.

Horts-Rittel, R. (2011) *The wicked problems project: teaching about wicked problems in leadership*. ebook at https://www.wickedproblems.ed.ac.uk

Koskinen, J., Zimmerman, J., and Binder, T. (2011) *Design research through practice*. Morgan Geneva: Elsevier Science & Technology.

Lucas, B. and Spencer, E. (2017) *Developing tenacity: teaching learners how to persevere in the face of difficulty*. Oxford : Heinemann.

McAleavy, T., Elwick, A. and Hall-Chen, A. (2019) *Sustaining success: high performing government schools in London*. Reading: Trust.

Midha , G. (2020) Time spent in unplanned meetings. The hidden gem in educational leadership. April 1, 2020 webmasterglobaled

Office for Economic Cooperation and Development (OECD). (2015) *Improving school leadership: policy and practice*. Brussels: OECD.

Raine, N. (2019) Unpublished research for MA in education – *How are schools using the pupil premium funding*. Oxford: Brookes University Library Resource.

Stogdill, R.M. (1974) *Handbook of leadership: a survey of theory and research* London: Free Press.

Turner, N., Barling, J., Epitropaki, O., Butcher, V. and Milner, O. (2013) *Transformational leadership and moral reasoning*. https://www.ncbi.nlm.nih.gov/pubmed/12002958

UNESCO (2014) *Education for all global monitoring report 2013/14: teaching and learning – achieving quality for all*. Paris: UNESCO.

Weber, E.P. and Khademian, A.M. (2008) Wicked problems, knowledge challenges, and collaborative capacity builders in network settings. *Public Administration Review*, 68, 334–349.

Weller, L.D. and Weller, S.J. (2002) *The assistant principal: essentials for effective school leadership.* Thousand Oaks, CA: Corwin P.

https://www.educationnews.org/international-uk/unesco-report-universal-primary-education-a-long-way-off/ (accessed 29th December, 2019)

www.newlandsacademy.org (accessed 20th May, 2020).

www.newmanschool.ofstedreport (accessed 20th May, 2020).

www.sportandthought.com (accessed 20th May, 2020).

www.sydneyrussell.org.uk (accessed 20th May, 2020).

www.staloysiusschool.org.com (accessed 20th May, 2020).

www.tallisschool.org.com (accessed 20th May, 2020).

www.trustforlondon.org.uk/data/boroughs/brent-poverty-and-inequality-indicators (accessed 20th May, 2020).

www.varndeancollege.org.com.uk (accessed 20th May, 2020).

9 Working with diversity

Effective schools are those that work in harmony and embrace difference, able to support learners and teachers from a range of backgrounds, with various cultures, political and social viewpoints, abilities and disabilities, status and gender membership. This chapter explores good practice in leadership for inclusion and reviews the theory associated with leading for diversity.

Active leadership needs to move beyond the mundane to adopt a world view which works collectively, with all peoples, to impact on global challenges. It needs to address humanitarian need and impact on spaces of exclusion and disconnect. Those spaces of exclusion and disconnect are many. They present themselves through expressions of 'otherness' and 'difference', and become visual when 'others' are excluded from leadership roles and when a leader fails to acknowledge the abilities and aptitudes of their staff. It is these two dimensions of exclusion that are the focus of this chapter, namely access to leadership roles and the requirement for leaders to embrace the cosmopolitan nature of our schools and offer opportunities for learners to thrive irrespective of their gender, race, ability or sexual orientation.

Firstly, access to leadership roles is explored with a specific focus given to issues of gender.

According to Morrison (2009),

> A view of schools as benign places, focused on equity in learning, and working for the good for all, must deliberately ignore evidence of the differentiated and inequitable pathways of learners, and the continuing exclusion of those deemed as 'other' from leadership roles.
>
> (Morrison, 2009:7–8)

It is essential that leadership models good practice embracing all citizens in our global reach and acknowledging the multiple elements of difference that constitute today's world.

The data in Table 9.1 illustrates the changing gender distribution of male and female teachers in the UK. It reveals an interesting picture with an increase in the percentage of men entering the profession at the primary phase between 1997 and 2012, with a small percentage decline in the most recent data, and a fluctuating picture at the secondary level. Overall the profession is still dominated by female workers yet, in terms of headship roles, males have increased their position annually for the last 11 years both in the primary and secondary age ranges. The British government had expressed concern over the shortage of men entering the primary phase of schooling, with special interventions designed to support and encourage male applications. This view formed part of the discourse of concern around societal breakdown where young people grow up without a male figurehead. In these circumstances male teachers, certainly at the primary phase, were considered important role models for young learners (https://www.theguardian.com/education/2008/sep/30/primaryschools.maleroles models).

The active promotion of men into the teaching profession has been contested and critiqued as promoting an inherent gender bias. Despite this, concern over the male role model and commonly held perceptions produced policy initiatives which encouraged men to take up teaching. From the following (perhaps 'available' would be better) data the strategies would appear to have worked with the percentage of men over women in primary teaching increasing year on year. What is disconcerting in the data is the low percentage of women in headship positions in the secondary age phase.

Research by Watterston (2019) has attempted to explain the lack of representation of women in leadership roles. Watterston's research highlighted that a significant component

Table 9.1 Percentage of men over women in primary and secondary teaching and headship

	1997		2004		2012		2018	
	Teachers	Heads	Teachers	Heads	Teachers	Heads	Teachers	Heads
Primary								
Men	11.7%	44.3%	12.2%	35.4%	13.1%	23.8%	20.1%	27.5%
Women	88.3%	55.7%	87.8%	64.6%	89.9%	71.2%	79.9%	63.5%
Secondary								
Men	46.4%	74.3%	42.7%	65.9%	39.9%	63.6%	38.5%	70.1%
Women	53.6%	25.7%	57.3%	34.1%	62.1%	36.4%	61.5%	29.9%

Source: www.dfe.workforcedata.gov.uk

of enabling greater diversity required women themselves to negate self-imposed barriers. This is supported by Morely (2013) who found that women are not or are rarely:

- Identified, supported and developed for leadership.
- Keen to achieve the most senior leadership positions in prestigious, national co-educational universities.
- Personally/collectively desiring of senior leadership.
- Attracted to labour intensity of competitive, audit cultures in the managerialised global academy.

(Morley, 2013)

In addition, Morley concluded that women are:

- Constrained by socio-cultural messages from entering middle management.
- Reluctant to enter some senior leadership positions.
- Often located on career pathways that do not lead to senior positions.
- Not attracted to influence, rewards and recognition.
- Feel burdened with emotional load.
  - Concerned about being 'other' in masculinist cultures.
  - Feel the pressure of navigating between professional and domestic responsibilities
- Often perceiving leadership as loss.
- Afraid of change.

(Morley, 2013:36)

Morley's research raises a number of key issues about women and their perceptions, not only in respect of their career trajectories but also the nature of leadership. Issues of societal pressure and a possible lack of confidence to move away from what is comfortable and achievable was an influencing element. Such perceptions align with stereotypical ideas about masculine and feminine behaviours and abilities. The leadership theories with the ambition to negate such ideas are the situational and contingency theories, where leadership styles and administrative contexts are perceived as gender neutral although some researchers maintain it is still apparent that:

- Women and men are judged differently (skill for a man is luck for a woman).
- Tasks may be identified as 'masculine' or 'feminine'.
- Definitions of task, skill, merit and competence is gender-biased.

(Blandford et al., 2017)

Research carried out by Smith (2015) identified gendered trends early in the teacher career trajectory by exploring the ambitions of final year teacher training students. She discovered that men rather than women were more likely to aspire to headship positions. Women tended to see themselves, if they aspired for promotion, in posts associated with special needs students – that is Special Educational Needs Co-ordinator (SENCO) roles. Smith (2015) reports that all research participants showed awareness of the challenges associated with leadership with male students more likely to see themselves in leadership positions in the future. Smith concludes her research report by stating: 'The under-representation of women in headship positions, and the shortages of aspirants to headship in general, continue to be issues schools need to address' (Smith, 2015:876).

Task 9.1 The cultural script of leadership

Do you think there are 'potent cultural templates or scripts' (Morley, 2013:117) about how leaders should be?

Is leadership a punishment as well as a reward (for example, the option of becoming a departmental leader in universities is not viewed positively by many researchers)?

Which of the following do you think explain women's absence from leadership roles?

- Gendered divisions of labour (e.g. childcare).
- Gender bias and misrecognition (i.e. valuing women less; being more critical of women leaders).
- Management and masculinities (i.e. assuming managers = male). (Is there a danger of stereotyping women positively as well as negatively, e.g. as caring, empathetic?).
- Greedy organisations (i.e. heavy workloads and too much stress).

Is leadership a gendered act?

To answer this question, we look in more detail at what have been classified as the 'situational theories of leadership', first proposed by Hersey and Blanchard (1969). These theories propose that the most effective style of leadership requires a leader to adapt their style and approach to different circumstances. Further, it is important to emphasise that there is no 'correct' leadership style. For example, some employees function better under a leader who is more autocratic and directive. For others, success will be more likely if the leader can step back and trust their team to make decisions and carry out plans without the leader's direct involvement. On a similar note, not all types of schools and locations require the same skills and leadership traits in equal measure. The required style might change over time as well. Some schools demand a large measure of innovation, whereas in others personal leadership, charisma and relational connection with staff are far more important.

Different theories have been developed that recognise the situational aspects of leadership. Each theory attempts to provide its own analysis of how leadership can be most successful in various situations.

Situational leadership theory

The term 'situational leadership' is most commonly derived from and connected with Hersey and Blanchard's situational leadership theory (1969). This approach to leadership proposes that leaders need to match two key leadership components appropriately: The leader's leadership style and the followers' maturity or preparedness levels.

The theory identifies four main leadership approaches:

- **Telling:** Directive and authoritative approach. The leader makes decisions and tells employees what to do.
- **Selling:** The leader is still the decision-maker, but they communicate and work to persuade the employees rather than simply directing them.
- **Participating:** The leader works with the team members to make decisions together. They support and encourage the team and are more democratic.
- **Delegating:** The leader assigns decision-making responsibility to team members but oversees their work.

In addition to these four approaches to leadership, there are also four levels of follower maturity, competence and commitment:

- **Level M1:** Followers have low competence and low commitment.
- **Level M2:** Followers have low competence, but high commitment.
- **Level M3:** Followers have high competence, but low commitment and confidence.
- **Level M4:** Followers have high competence and high commitment and confidence.

In Hersey and Blanchard's approach the key to successful leadership is matching the correct leadership style to the corresponding maturity level of the staff. It is proposed that each of the four leadership styles is appropriate for the corresponding employee maturity level:

- Telling style works best for leading employees at the M1 level (low competence, low commitment).
- Selling style works best for leading employees at the M2 level (low competence, high commitment).

- Participating style works best for leading employees at the M3 level (high competence, low commitment/confidence).
- Delegating style works best for leading employees at the M4 level (high competence, high commitment/confidence).

In an education context it is likely that most colleagues in a working environment will have high competence and knowledge about their subject and indeed the act of teaching. They may lack confidence early in their careers in respect of the specific context of the educational environment in which they are working.

Identifying the employee maturity level becomes a very important part of the process, and the leader must have the willingness and ability to use any of the four leadership styles as needed.

Goleman's model of situational leadership

Another situational theory of leadership developed by Goleman incorporates the concept of emotional intelligence. Goleman postulates six categories of situational leadership, describing each leadership style and suggesting when this style is most appropriate and likely to be successful:

Pacesetting Leader	The leader sets aggressive goals and standards and drives employees to reach them. This works with highly motivated and competent employees, but can lead to burnout due to the high energy demands and stress levels.
Authoritative Leader	The leader authoritatively provides a direction and goals for the team, expecting the team to follow their lead. The details are often left up to the team members. This works well when clear direction is needed, but can be problematic if the team members are highly experienced and knowledgeable and might resent interference.
Affiliative Leader	A positive reinforcement and morale-boosting style. The leader praises and encourages the employees, refraining from criticism or reprimand. The goal is to foster team bonding and connectedness, along with a sense of belonging. This approach works best in times of stress and trauma or when trust needs to be rebuilt. It is not likely to be sufficient as a long-term or exclusive strategy.
Coaching Leader	The leader focuses on helping individual employees build their skills and develop their talents. This approach works best when employees are receptive to guidance and willing to hear about their weaknesses and where they need to improve.
Democratic Leader	The leader intentionally involves followers in the decision-making process by seeking their opinion and allowing them a voice in the final decision. This works well when the leader is in need of guidance and/or the employees are highly qualified to contribute and there are not strenuous time constraints that require quick decisions.
Coercive Leader	The leader acts as the ultimate authority and demands immediate compliance with directions, even applying pressure as needed. This can be appropriate in times of crisis or disaster, but is not advisable in healthy situations.

(Adapted from Goleman, 2013).

Consider the following case study, anonymised at the request of the headteacher.

Case study 9.1 Large academy in Lancashire

Mary was appointed as the head of a large academy converter school in the Lancashire and North Yorkshire Area. During the interview she met the acting deputy head who appeared confident that he would be appointed to a full-time post, having described the interview process to all applicants as a 'formality'! This was Mary's first headship and she anticipated some resentment from the displaced acting head. Her first act as head was to meet with her leadership team, which consisted of three men and one woman.

Roles and responsibilities in the school were divided on a traditional gendered basis with the female deputy responsible for safeguarding, pastoral care, looked-after children, young carers, social service liaison and attendance. The male deputies had responsibility for issues such as discipline, uniform compliance, timetabling, room allocation, cover arrangements, links with local primary schools, transition arrangements, school-to-school partnerships and external liaison. Mary created a list of all these roles and decided to bring her leadership team together to discuss with them, collaboratively, the nature of each role asking them to determine how much time they spent on each task on a weekly basis. She then asked the team if they wanted to consider a change in role. This collaborative exercise she carried out using an affiliative approach, acknowledging the good work underway whilst also using a coaching model to determine what her team really wanted from their leadership role. By modelling the approaches already identified (Goldman's situational theory) Mary had the information she needed to restructure her leadership team and offer new areas of challenge to all her senior staff. As a possible spinoff from this approach going forward the leadership team worked well together and the deputy head, who had not been successful in his application, gained a headship elsewhere having broadened his repertoire of experience and skills.

Task 9.2 Your leadership journey

In the light of Goleman's categories of leadership listed, consider specific occasions in your journey to leadership, or in your current leadership role, when you have used the styles as identified or observed others using them. Consider the impact and evaluate whether the approach was appropriate for the situation and the intended outcome.

It is strongly argued that providing women and girls with equal access to education, health care, rewarding work and representation in political and economic decision-making processes will grow economies and benefit societies and humanity at large. Implementing new legal frameworks regarding female equality in the workplace and the eradication of harmful practices targeted at women is crucial to ending the gender-based discrimination prevalent in many countries around the world. But this call must apply to all disadvantaged groups irrespective of gender, ethnicity or sexual orientation.

Focusing on ethnicity

The Department for Education data reveals that 94.4% of headteachers are white British, leaving 5.6% with a non-white-British heritage (www.dfes.workforce.data) (Table 9.2 below).

Related to issues of ethnicity the work of Woods and colleagues on 'democratic' leadership offers an appropriate approach and one which 'entails rights to meaningful participation and respect for and expectations towards everyone as ethical beings' (Woods et al., 2004).

The democratic leadership style is based on mutual respect. It is often combined with participatory leadership because it requires collaboration between leaders and the people they guide. This operates in two ways:

1. Democratic leaders expect people who report to them to have in-depth experience and to exhibit self-confidence.
2. Democratic leaders are involved in the decision-making process.

The democratic leadership approach requires trust, responsibility, honest brokerage of decision making and the ability to make and be able to justify fair and reasoned decisions. Furthermore, this applies when working with staff teams as well as pupils.

Table 9.2 Distribution by ethnic membership

	Teachers	Headteachers
White British	88.4%	94.4%
Other white	3.3%	
White Irish	1.6%	
Indian	1.3%	
Other	5.4%	

When working with student democratic leaders encourage a school culture which:

- Identifies and celebrates individual and generic differences.
- Acknowledges the skill of all children.
- Shows support for difference.
- Understands the impact of difference.
- Empathises with children, to understand their view.
- Provides for difference.
- Celebrates diversity.
- Recognises uniqueness.

Headteachers employing these approaches exercise 'leadership with emancipatory intent' (Fuller, 2012, p. 686). Although, according to Morrison et al. (2007:19), 'Education leaders appear to be more willing to consider diversity among learners than to consider diversity among leaders or staff as an issue of social justice' and, according to Courtney (2014), individuals link socially to those like themselves. If staff are supported in their gender nonconformity then so will students feel supported.

Researchers advocate three productive leadership practices that increase equity, namely:

- A common vision about the significance of equity and how it might be pursued.
- Supportive social relations between staff.
- Dispersed leadership practices.

(Niesche and Keddie, 2011:74)

'A leadership grounded in inclusion and equity reflects an imperative to facilitate access, engagement and the full and active membership of a defined community' (Rayner, 2008:46).

Task 9.3 Reflection

Consider:

- To what extent have you experienced equitable leadership practices?
- Do you agree that the three practices described are likely to increase equity?
- What else needs to be done?

Embracing difference in the curriculum

In 2014 the British government published the 'Public Sector Equality Duty Guidance' for schools in England, which required schools to acknowledge the rich diversity of the modern world to prepare our youth for life in modern Britain. This included teaching about lesbian, gay, bisexual and transgendered (LGBT) people as well as those still exploring or questioning their identity (LGBTQ+). According to research carried out by Stonewall, the society for supporting LGBTQ+ citizens, nearly half of all LGBT pupils experience bullying of some form (www.stonewall.org.uk).

For school leaders this requires diligence and a willingness to challenge discriminatory language and actions. It also demands curriculum approaches which allow children to learn about LGBT issues from a formative age, and to encourage strong friendships from a young age, irrespective of gender identity. This creates an environment that promotes compassion and respect for children and adults in the school setting.

The following welcome section is taken from the website of the Charles Dickens primary school in London.

Case study 9.2 Charles Dickens primary school

Families come in all shapes and sizes. Some children have a mum and a dad, others live with their grandparents and some children have two mums or two dads.

There are now almost 20,000 children growing up in same-sex parent families and many children have lesbian, gay, bisexual and trans parents or family. Children will learn better and will be more engaged if they find their families reflected in class and they will grow up to be more successful learners, confident individuals, and responsible citizens.

In order to prepare children for the diverse society they live in and to prevent poor behaviour and bullying, it is important to talk about difference in general and different families in particular. At Charles Dickens School, we learn about and celebrate different family structures within our PSHE scheme of work. All children learn about the many different family structures and encouraged to talk positively about their own. In Key Stage Two, we use the Stonewall resources, including the videos, to explore identity including same-sex relationships and gender. These age-appropriate explore the stories of four different children. If you are interested in finding out more there is an option to register as a pupil on the Stonewall Primary site to access further materials and information videos.

Task 9.4 Good practice audit

Carry out a 'good practice' audit in your school and identify all aspects of the school which promote a culture of acceptance and support for difference. Review, for example, the school's mission and values and the presentation of images on the website and in corridors and classroom walls. Is the curriculum balanced, is a range of literature used which embraces the rich diversity of the country we live in?

In Massachusetts, USA, an advocacy movement among secondary aged pupils, known as the Gay, Lesbian and Straight Educational Network (GLSEN, pronounced 'glisten') and aimed at promoting 'gay/straight alliances', is gaining momentum.

Presenting itself as a civil rights organisation concerned with 'tolerance' and 'understanding' for a victim group, it seeks to transform the culture and instruction of every school in America.

The organisations handbook states that middle-schoolers 'should have the freedom to explore [their] sexual orientation and find [their] own unique expression of lesbian, bisexual, gay, straight, or any combination of these' (www.glsen.org.usa). One of the major goals of GLSEN is to reform public school curricula and teaching so that LGBTQ+ themes are always central and always presented in the approved light.

The group call for every course in every public school to focus on LGBTQ+ issues. The group help identify appropriate and accessible resources such as the following books for the early years classroom: *One Dad, Two Dads, Brown Dad, Blue Dads, King and King* and *Asha's Mums* (www.glsen.org.usa).

As a leader it is important to embrace issues of LGBTQ+ in relation to staff and students. The following chart offers some advice in terms of appropriate language to use. Universities are responding in various ways with Oxford Brookes University offering training to staff and students, producing a policy, setting up a diversity committee with member representation from LGBTQ+ staff and students, and offering staff who are LGBTQ+ allies a lanyard to wear.

The diversity committee has produced the Table 9.3 to illustrate the appropriate language to use when discussing LGBTQ+ matters. This approach is extremely helpful as a step towards encouraging conversations whilst supporting participants to engage thoughtfully and respectfully.

Table 9.3 LGBTQ+ inclusive language, dos and don'ts

AVOID SAYING	SAY INSTEAD	WHY?	EXAMPLE
'Hermaphrodite'	'Intersex'	Hermaphrodite is a stigmatising, inaccurate word with a negative medical history.	'What are the best practices for the medical care of intersex infants?'
'Homosexual'	'Gay'	'Homosexual' often connotes a medical diagnosis, or a discomfort with gay/lesbian people.	'We want to do a better job of being inclusive of our gay employees'.
'Born female' or 'born male'	'Assigned female/male at birth'	'Assigned' language accurately depicts the situation of what happens at birth.	'Max was assigned female at birth, then he transitioned in high school'.
'Female-bodied' or 'male-bodied'	'Assigned female/male at birth'	'Bodied' language is often interpreted as pressure to medically transition, or invalidation of one's gender identity.	'Max was assigned female at birth, then he transitioned in high school'.
'A gay' or 'a transgender'	'A gay/transgender person'	Gay and transgender are adjectives that describe a person/group.	'We had a transgender athlete in our league this year'.
'Transgender people and normal people'	'Transgender people and cisgender people'	Saying 'normal' implies 'abnormal'. Which is a stigmatising way to refer to a person.	'This group is open to transgender and cisgender people'.
'Both genders' or 'opposite sexes'	'All genders'	'Both' implies there are only two; 'opposite' reinforces antagonism amongst genders.	'Video games aren't just a boy thing – kids of all genders play them'.
'Ladies and gentlemen'	'Everyone', 'Folks', 'Honoured guests', etc.	Moving away from binary language is more inclusive of people of all genders.	'Good morning everyone: Next stop Piccadilly Station'.
'Mailman', 'fireman', 'policeman', etc.	'Mail clerk', 'Firefighter', 'Police officer', etc.	People of all genders do these jobs.	'I actually saw a fire fighter rescue a cat from a tree'.
'It' when referring to someone (e.g. when pronouns are unknown)	'They'	'It' is for referring to things, not people.	'You know, I am not sure how they identify'.

Rights-respecting schools

Schools in the UK are able to apply for the kitemark as rights-respecting institutions as designated by the United Nations Convention for the Rights of the Child. The UN articles of convention stipulate that every child should be valued, cared for and developed to their full potential.

Case study 9.3 Audley primary school

Audley primary school in London is a rights-respecting school and proud of the badge of honour it has been given. The school website states:

Our aims, values and pledge support the ambitions of the UNICEF Recognition of Commitment to the Rights Respecting Schools Award. We are now on our journey to becoming a rights-based community in which children are valued and where they are able to thrive. We reflect the belief that the United Nations Convention of the Rights of the Child (CRC) '…gives young people the best chance to grow into respectful, active and resilient citizens' www.audleyprimaryschool.gov.uk.

Also, on the school website is a questionnaire for staff and governors to complete as part of their commitment to the rights of the children who attend Audley (Table 9.4 below). This can act as an awareness-raising activity for new staff and those connected with the school.

So, what is the 'Rights Respecting Schools Award'?

The Rights Respecting School Award is an initiative run by UNICEF UK which encourages schools to place the UN Convention on the Rights of the Child at the heart of their ethos and curriculum. A rights-respecting School not only teaches about children's rights; it also models rights and respect in all its relationships, whether between children or between children and adults.

In Surrey a school that is also a rights-respecting school has appointed school ambassadors among its pupils.

Table 9.4 Questionnaire to confirm perceptions

STAFF AND GOVERNOR QUESTIONNAIRE

SCHOOL NAME:

JOB TITLE:

Tick the box to show how far you agree, strongly agree, agree, disagree, strongly disagree or are not sure.

1. In general, I am treated with respect by other adults in the school.
2. In general, I am treated with respect by pupils in the school.
3. I feel comfortable talking to pupils about their rights.
4. I enjoy working at this school.
5. In general, pupils are actively engaged in the life of the school.
6. Pupils can influence decisions made in the school.

Task 9.5 Consider children's rights

Consider the tensions and uncertainties in the VUCA world we inhabit. What value can the commitment of a school to be a rights-respecting school add to the security and stability of the children who attend it?

The competencies covered in this chapter which form part of the National Professional Qualification for Leadership are:

Present, communicate or defend challenging messages confidently and positively to a range of audiences.
 Anticipate other peoples' views or feelings and moderate your approach accordingly.

References

Blandford, E., Brill, C., Neave, S. and Roberts, A. (2017) *Equality in higher education: statistical report 2011.* London: HESA – Equality Challenge.

Courtney, S. (2014) Developing school leaders of diverse school types. *American Leadership Research Association USA: Philadelphia Conference Paper* 21st .May, 2014 –Philadelphia.

Goldman, D. (2013) *Leadership: the power of emotional intelligence.* Nottingham, MA: More Than Summer Publishing.

Hersey, P. and Blanchard, K.H. (1969) *Management of organizational behaviour,* 3rd ed – *Utilizing human resources.* New Jersey: Prentice Hall.

https://www.theguardian.com/education/2008/sep/30/primaryschools.malerolemodels (accessed 20th May, 2020).

Morley, L. (2013) International trends in women's leadership in higher education. In Stiasny, M. and Gore, T. (eds.) *Going global: identifying the trends and drivers of international education.* Oxford: Heinemann, pp. 672–681.

Morrison, M. (2009) *Leadership and learning matters for social justice.* London: Information Age Publishing.

Niesche, R. and Keddie, A. (2011) Foregrounding issues of equity and diversity in educational leadership. *School Leadership and Management,* 31 (1), 65–77.

Rayner, S. (2008) Complexity, diversity and management. Some reflections on folklore and learning leadership in education. *Management in Education,* 22 (2), 40–46.

Smith, J. (2015) Gendered trends in student teachers' professional aspirations. *Journal of Educational Management Administration and Leadership*, 43 (6), 861–882.

Watterston, B. (2019) *Step in, step up: empowering women for the school leadership journey.* Sydney, NSW: Australia Press.

Woods, P.A., Bennett, N., Harvey, J.A. and Wise, C. (2004) Variabilities and dualities in distributed leadership: findings from a systematic literature review. *Educational Management Administration and Leadership*, 32 (4), 439–57.

www.charlesdickensschool.gov.uk (accessed 20th May, 2020).

www.dfe.workforcedata.gov.uk (accessed 20th May, 2020).

www.glsen.org.usa (accessed 20th May, 2020).

www.stonewall.org.uk (accessed 20th May, 2020).

10 Leading continuing professional development

Significant attention has been given to the preparation and development of school leaders with government initiatives in the Western world focused on building a world-class education system. Many nations including England have established a system of accreditation with a mandatory level of qualification for leadership roles. In addition, the role of the school leader now encompasses responsibility for the training of staff where once centrally offered courses, from government-approved organisations, offered national support and training. The demise of central support has occurred as major policy change has impacted the school sector with new curricula, policy changes and an increase in legislative requirements. What has developed is a 'do it yourself' regional model for continuing professional development (CPD) with additional expectations placed on school leaders. Policy change in other jurisdictions is explored with a focus on work underway in Israel and Africa which identifies the need for leaders to be 'sense-makers' as competing expectations create tensions for those charged with delivering CPD. This chapter models the approach adopted when instructional leadership becomes the main thrust as the approach most likely to support leaders, particularly when taking responsibility for the CPD dimension of teachers' lives.

The English qualification system

In the English system aspiring leaders are expected to complete a range of qualifications linked to leadership ambition and career progression. To this end the requirements for qualification as middle leaders, senior leaders, headship and executive leadership are set out on the DfE website.

Attempts have been made at the end of every chapter in this text to map content and the suggested tasks to the coverage of the National Professional Qualification (NPQ) criteria which cover six areas of content, namely:

1. Strategy and improvement.
2. Teaching and curriculum excellence.
3. Leading with impact.
4. Working in partnership.
5. Managing resources and risks.
6. Increasing capability.

(DfE, 2014)

For those aspiring to be a headteacher the following is required:

- Taking part in a placement in another school for at least nine days.
- Leading a school change programme, lasting at least two terms, to improve pupil progress and attainment.
- Designing an action plan to meet the placement school's resourcing and capability needs.

(DfE, 2014)

These criteria make it very clear that headship requires experience beyond your existing school, the ability to lead change that will impact at the point of learner progress and achievement and the ability to design plans which focus on resourcing and financial viability.

The Importance of CPD

The importance of teacher and leader involvement in developmental opportunities has been emphasised in the academic literature and aligned closely with fostering an improvement culture in our schools. It is highlighted for the part it plays in maintaining and enhancing the quality of teaching and learning (Craft, 2000; Harland and Kinder,1997; Harris, 2001). Research has shown that professional development is an essential component of successful school level change and development (Day, 1999; Hargreaves, 2012) and has confirmed that where teachers are able to access new ideas and to share experiences more readily, there is greater potential for school and classroom improvement. Evidence also suggests that attention to teacher learning can impact directly upon improvements in student learning and achievement. Where teachers expand and develop their own teaching repertoires and are clear in their purposes, it is more likely that they will provide an increased range of learning opportunities for students (Joyce et al., 1998). Further, the research literature demonstrates that professional development can have a positive impact on curriculum and pedagogy, as well as teachers' sense of commitment and their relationships with students (Talbert and McLaughlin, 1994).

Participation in CPD has been found to support teachers and leaders to stay in role, giving them confidence in their practice and the opportunity to share concerns and learn from others (Priestley et al., 2015). The very act of meeting other leaders in the same predicament, in an environment away from the school, allows for in-confidence conversations that can support the failing or tired teacher (Sachs, 2003). Allowing teachers to attend training at a distance away from the pressure of everyday teaching, to attend a local university for example, as an independent professional, was found to be empowering. The anonymity of training with others to share experiences in confidence has been identified as a key element of successful school improvement (Gray, 2000; Harris, 2002; Maden and Hillman, 1996; OfSTED, 2014). This particular focus on the benefit of CPD experienced away from the place of employment is relevant given that the newly determined models of local partnership in the form of teaching school alliances make it more likely that training is delivered in school with school leaders and colleagues 'in the room'.

Researchers have tried, over a number of years, to measure the impact of educational interventions by trying to record value for money spent on CPD as a means of improving teaching and student learning (Brew, 2007; Devlin, 2008; Gosling, 2008; Chalmers et al., 2012). Measurement has focused on the short-, medium- and long-term affects with particular attention given to how engagement in CPD has impacted student learning and the internal environment of the participating institutions. Trigwell (2012) suggests that using school-based data that are already collected through the official publicly available sources such as Raise-On-line offers an in-depth additional lens through which to consider impact and may well provide a longitudinal perspective. This could be methodologically problematic since it would be difficult to attribute student learning gain to any one specific element of CPD although attempts to create stronger associations might be achieved in the way the CPD is designed and targeted.

Task 10.1 Pupil achievement

Think about something in your own school that might benefit teachers and could be introduced as CPD. Link the proposed CPD to an element of pupil achievement.

International approaches

Research by Eacott and Asuga (2014) has highlighted the problematic nature of leadership training in Africa. Here, models of training still rely on the traditional approaches of the colonial days when ideas and expertise were borrowed from the Western world. This they maintain is no longer appropriate, arguing that the African education system needs to ask new questions and construct alternative narratives specific to the African context.

In a similar vein, Moorosi critiques existing training programmes for leadership in Africa for their patriarchal design and content. Moorosi (2014) notes the gender inequity in leadership positions in her country whilst identifying the complex intersection of gender, race, context and background that influence the outcomes of leadership development programmes, with women still denied equal access and chances to succeed. Issues of gendered access to leadership are addressed in Chapter 9.

Whether in the UK or further afield, the knowledge and skills teachers need to be effective as leaders largely lie beyond what most learn in their teacher preparation programmes. This includes knowledge of building a community, sharing ownership, managing numerous groups, facilitating dialogue, leading professional learning, guiding evidence-based decision-making, systems thinking, communication, advocacy and self-care.

By expanding our understanding of the varied ways in which increasing numbers of teachers are learning to lead, we may be able to envision potential new opportunities for learning and leadership in schools. It is worth considering what kind of opportunities can be designed to enhance teachers' capacities to influence each other in formal and informal ways.

In the US, the Consortium for Policy Research in Education has mapped the landscape of programmes and initiatives that support teacher leaders. The research assessed nearly 300 programs that support teachers to take on new and varied roles (Berg et al., 2019).

The research revealed that the available programmes were designed to support teachers to be leaders in one or more of the following three ways:

1. They prepared teachers to lead through professional learning designed to help them build the knowledge and skills they needed to be influential beyond their classrooms.
2. They placed teachers in formal leadership positions that gave them a vantage point for guiding their peers.
3. They recognised teachers for possessing valued knowledge, skills or dispositions and held them up as examples for others to follow.

Forward-thinking schools plan ahead and think about building individual expertise in ways that are organisationally useful, what is regularly referred to as 'succession planning' but infrequently practised. Strengthening the capacity of school teams can be very advantageous (Johnson, 2019) for long-term recruitment planning.

Leaders taking responsibility for CPD

As mentioned in the introduction to this chapter headteachers in the English education system now have the responsibility for ensuring that their staff are trained and qualified to address the changing requirements of teaching.

According to the standards for teachers' professional development, teacher CPD needs to:

1. Be focused on improving and evaluating pupil outcomes.
2. Be underpinned by robust evidence and expertise.
3. Include collaboration and expert challenge.
4. Be sustained over time.
5. Be prioritised by leadership.

(DfE, 2015)

The final point is the key one for leaders. There is an expectation that school leaders should be actively involved in staff training plans with relevant courses 'prioritised by leadership'.

The leadership of learning is not just a leadership dimension that occurs in the English system. Robinson (2011) conducted research across 23 countries to identify key factors of effective school leadership in relation to improving learning. This research identified that teacher development has the biggest impact on students. However, many headteachers claimed that they spend 'too little time' on the leadership of teaching and learning; only 40% engaged in the research felt the time spent was about right (Robinson, 2011). To address the pressures of leadership some headteachers have appointed leadership posts as part of the senior leadership team with a member of staff responsible for teaching and learning. This approach illustrates distributed leadership in action, whilst headteachers who take action to engage fully in the CPD arrangements for their staff might be categorised as adopting an instructional or pedagogic leadership style. Whichever model is adopted school size will influence what a headteacher can do.

Southworth (2011) advocates instructional leadership for schools facing challenges. Here the headteacher is conceptualised as the 'lead learner' with learning occurring at a number of levels: Pupil, adult and organisation. School leaders can direct efforts to improve staff and student learning through a number of strategies:

- Observing teachers in the classroom, reviewing lesson plans and discussing lesson objectives.
- Walking around the school regularly and 'dropping in' to classrooms, laboratories and sports areas.
- Holding regular staff meetings where teaching, learning and pupil progress is the main agenda item.
- Making sure teacher performance reviews, as required in the English system, are targeted and well-planned, setting objectives and new challenges on an annual basis.
- Offering additional support where or when required.
- Setting interclass challenges to see which class can achieve the most awards and thereby motivating teachers.
- Establishing expectations on a regular basis around wall displays and the presentation of work in the school corridors and reception area.

The following case study illustrates the role that positive rewards can play in the leadership challenge. The process is evidence of a leader concerned about school discipline, prepared to be involved whilst offering support to her staff.

Case study 10.1 Award systems

When Mary took over the leadership of a failing school she was shocked at the number of exclusions, detentions and 'penalty points' allocated to the students which seemed to pervade the operation of the school. Large numbers of pupils were sent to sit outside her office on a daily basis and it was clear that, for some learners, they did not even know why they were there.

She decided to shift the focus away from the negative and to reward the positive. She instigated a system of rewards: Bronze, Silver and Gold, topped off with Welsh Gold which was to be a very special reward acknowledging at the end of the year those children who had excelled. The system was introduced to the staff, who were initially very sceptical. Quite quickly the number of children sent to the head for disciplinary purposes changed to be replaced by children arriving with good work to show, with notes about acts of kindness to others and requests for acknowledgements for good behaviour.

In her first year as headteacher Mary distributed 350 Bronze Awards, 210 Silver, 106 Gold and 5 Welsh Gold. The number of pupil suspensions reduced to nil and only four pupils had to be excluded from the classroom for a short period of time.

Here is an example of atomic leadership in action. Mary identified a problem after a very brief time in the school. She introduced a small change which in time had a dramatic impact on the school. By creating an orderly and learner-focused environment, Mary gave her teachers time to focus on teaching and learning in a positive way.

There are other structural changes that leadership teams might consider to support school staff, particularly those working in challenging circumstances who might not be motivated to engage and commit to CPD:

1. Leaders might review the amount of time pupils spend on particular tasks. Is the lunch break too long, for example, leading to pupil boredom and low concentration in the afternoon?
2. Review the membership of different classes for various subjects. Look at gender distribution, ethnicity and age. Are there distribution issues in these areas that might be adding pressure in the classroom?
3. Use discretionary money, where available, to encourage and enhance innovative activity.
4. Influence the working patterns of teachers by rearranging physical space and 'free' time to promote new forms of collegiality and experimentation.
5. Foster agreement about the level of teacher expectation needed to encourage higher levels of pupil motivation whilst also having a realistic understanding of what can be achieved.
6. Facilitate debate about what counts as a 'good lesson', what theories of learning are appropriate to the achievement of particular objectives and the form of feedback pupils should receive to help them understand what is an acceptable performance.

(Adapted and developed from the work of Earley and Higham, 2002)

Case study 10.2 Thomas Reade Primary School

The staffroom at Thomas Reade Primary School in Abingdon contains a whiteboard upon which staff can leave notes to one another about school events. As an illustration of the collegial approach in this learning-centred school, the following was posted on the whiteboard:

I am trying to deliver the Key Stage 1 curriculum for Mathematics (the section on fractions). I have used paper, I have introduced shapes to be coloured in, I have cut up sandwiches. Does anyone have any other ideas please? There are a few children in the class who are really struggling with this.

133

Leadership theory

A number of leadership theories might be applied to better understand and support leaders involved in planning and delivering CPD to their staff. The most appropriate one is that of instructional leadership as one of the most enduring models of leadership theory (Hallinger, 2003). Instructional leadership is focused on improving teaching and learning and as such is primarily about the direction of leaders' influence, which is targeted at school improvement.

Instructional leadership has three core constituents which have been adapted over time:

1. Defining a clear mission.
2. Managing programmes of teaching and learning.
3. Promoting a positive school climate.

(Hallinger, 2003)

More recent research has broadened the focus of instructional leadership to include collaboration among teachers, providing opportunities for professional growth and the development of professional learning communities (Silva et al., 2011). Instructional leadership is interested in a 'direct effect' approach to highlighting the relationship between leadership practices and student achievement.

The competencies from the National Professional Qualifications for Leadership covered in that chapter are:

> Support all members of the team with appropriate and targeted opportunities for professional development.
>
> Evaluate the impact of professional development on teacher development and pupil outcomes.
>
> Design professional development strategies which engage all staff (including newly/recently qualified teachers) and anticipate future professional development needs.

 # References

Berg, J.H., Horn, P., Supovitz, J. and Margolis, J. (2019) *Typology of teacher leadership programs (Research Report #RR 2019-1)*. Philadelphia, PA: Consortium for Policy Research in Education, University of Pennsylvania.

Brew, A. (2007) Evaluating academic development in a time of perplexity. *International Journal for Academic Development*, 12, 69–72.

Chalmers, D., Stoney, S., Goody, A., Goerke, V. and Gardiner, D. (2012) *Identification and implementation of indicators and measures of effectiveness of teaching preparation programmes in higher education.* Canberra, ACT: Australian Government. Office for Learning and Teaching.

Craft, A. (2000) *Continuing professional development: a practical guide for teachers and schools.* 2nd ed. London: Routledge Falmer.

Day, C. (1999) Professional development and reflective practice: purposes, processes and partnerships. *Pedagogy, Culture and Society,* 7 (2), 221–233.

Department for Education. (2014) A world-class teaching profession. https://www.gov.uk/government/publications/a-world-class-teaching-profession (accessed 13.1.2020).

Department for Education. (2015) *Standards for teacher development.* Norwich: Her Majesties Stationery Office.

Devlin, M. (2008) Research challenges inherent in determining improvement in university teaching. *Issues in Educational Research,* 18, 12–25.

Eacott, S. and Asuga, G. (2014) School leadership preparation and development in Africa. *Journal of Educational Management Administration and Leadership,* 42 (6), 919–927.

Earley, P. and Higham, R. (2012) *Review of the school leadership landscape.* Nottingham: NCSL.

Gosling, D. (2008) *Educational development in the United Kingdom. Report for the heads of educational development group.* London: Heads of Educational Development Group (HEDG). Retrieved 20th October 2014 from: http://www.hedg.ac.uk/documents/HEDG_Report_final.pdf

Gray, J. (2000) *Causing concern but improving: a review of schools' experience.* London: DfEE.

Hallinger, P. (2003) Leading educational change. Reflections on the practice of instructional and transformational leadership. *Cambridge Journal of Education,* 33, 329–351.

Hargreaves, D.H. (2012) *A self-improving school system in international context.* Nottingham: National College for School Leadership.

Harris, A. (2001) Building the capacity for school improvement. *School Leadership and Management,* 21 (3), 261–270.

Harland, J. and Kinder, K. (1997) 'Teachers' continuing professional development: framing a model of outcomes. *British Journal of In-Service Education,* 23 (1), 71–84.

Johnson, S.M. (2019) *Where teachers thrive: organizing schools for success.* Cambridge, MA: Harvard Education Press.

Joyce, B. and Calhoun, E. (1998) *Models of teaching: tools for learning.* Buckingham: Open University Press.

Maden, M. and Hillman, J. (1996) *Success against the odds.* London: Routledge.

Moorosi, P. (2014) Constructing a leader's identity through a leadership development programme: an intersectional analysis. School leadership preparation and development in Africa. *Journal of Educational Management Administration and Leadership,* 42 (6), 792–807.

OfSTED. (2014) *Improving city schools*. London: Office for Standards in Education.

Priestley, M., Biesta, G.J.J., Philippou, S. and Robinson, S. (2015) The teacher and the curriculum: exploring teacher agency. In D. Wyse, L. Hayward, and J. Pandya (eds.) *The SAGE handbook of curriculum, pedagogy and assessment*. London: SAGE Publications Ltd. Higher Education OUP Humanities & Social Sciences Study 27.

Robinson, V. (2011) *Student centred leadership*. San Francisco, CA: Jose Bass.

Sachs, J. (2003) *The activist teaching professional*. Buckinghamshire: Open University Press.

Silva, J., White, G. and Yoshida, R. (2011) The direct effects of principal-student discussions on eighth grade students' gains in reading achievement: a experimental study. *Educational Administration Quarterly*, 47, 722–793.

Southworth, G. (2011) Connecting leadership and learning. In Robinson, J. and Timperley, H. (eds.) *Leadership and learning*. London: SAGE.

Talbert, J.E. and McLaughlin, M.W. (1994) Teacher professionalism in local school contexts. *American Journal of Education*, 102 (2), 123–153.

Trigwell, K. (2012) Variation in the experience of leadership of teaching in higher education. *Studies in Higher Education*, 28 (3), 247–259.

PART IV

Leadership with responsibility

Global challenges, school attendance, teacher and leader supply

The United Nations' Sustainable Development Goals aspire to an education for all children 3–11 years old irrespective of race, culture, identity or status by 2030. One of the keys to achieving this ambition will be the training and retention of high-quality teaching staff.

There is currently a severe shortage of teachers across the world. To address this many leaders of education are approaching classroom teaching in different ways with teachers using job sharing, flexible working contracts and other flexible working approaches. This chapter looks at leadership approaches to offering flexible working opportunities whilst protecting the work/life balance of the staff and the leadership team.

Sustainable Development Goals

The United Nations' Sustainable Development Goals aspire to a quality education as the foundation to creating sustainable development. In addition to improving quality of life, access to inclusive education can help equip people with the skills required to develop innovative solutions to the world's greatest problems.

At the beginning of the second decade of the second millennium over 265 million children are currently out of school and 22% of them are of primary school age. Many children who are attending schools are lacking basic skills in reading and math. In the past decade, major progress had been made towards increasing access to education at all levels and increasing enrolment rates in schools particularly for women and girls. Basic literacy skills have improved but greater efforts are needed to make even larger strides towards achieving universal education goals.

The reasons for the restricted access to a quality education are a lack of adequately trained teachers, poor conditions of schools and equity issues in respect of the opportunities provided to rural children. For quality education to be provided to the children of impoverished families investment is needed in educational scholarships, teacher training workshops, school building and improvement of water and electricity access in schools.

Data from UNESCO have identified a teacher shortage of mass proportion across the globe, with resultant pressures on the UNESCO 2030 ambitions that all children below the age of 11 should be in full-time education. Here we explore the seriousness of the situation before focusing on research carried out in England identifying the different ways in which leaders are retaining high-performing colleagues even in schools operating in challenging circumstances.

Published data from the UNESCO Institute for Statistics (UIS) shows that if the current trend continues, 33 countries will not have enough teachers to provide quality education to all children by 2030. Specifically, by 2030:

- 33 countries will still not have enough teachers to provide every child with a primary education.
- 25.8 million school teachers need to be recruited worldwide to provide every child with a primary education, which includes 3.2 million new posts and the replacement of 22.6 million teachers expected to leave the profession.

Publication of this data by UNESCO as aligned to the achievement of Sustainable Development Goal 4 (SDG 4) has led to specific calls on countries to significantly increase the recruitment and training of teachers to the profession. That said, those working in the profession still remain undervalued in terms of both pay and societal respect.

In the UK there are more female teachers overall than male. This is not the case worldwide with a shortage of teachers – particularly female – where they are most needed, in rural communities. In India, the share of female teachers declines with the remoteness of schools, from 60% when the school is located in the local government area and to 30% when it is 30 km away.

More teachers are needed in displaced settings. If all refugee children enrolled for schooling, Turkey would need 80,000 additional teachers, Germany would need 42,000 teachers and educators and Uganda would need 7,000 additional primary teachers. Yet refugee teachers are often excluded from national training programmes because of professional regulations on the right to work. In many displacement settings, safety concerns and cultural practices result in a shortage of female staff. The share of female primary teachers was 10% at Dadaab camp, Kenya, in 2016, and 16% at Dollo Ado camp, Ethiopia, in 2014 (UNESCO: Global Education Monitoring Report, 2018).

A report in *UK Times Newspaper* (26/9/18) titled 'Exodus of teachers is a lesson for politicians' identifies another part of the teacher supply spectrum in that even when teachers are trained, they don't stay in the profession. In the UK the school-aged population is set to grow by 11% in the next decade and teachers are complaining en masse about the pressures they are under. In 2018 just under 40,000 left the profession and about 9% of the workforce left in 2016. There is a predicted shortfall of 30,000 classroom teachers in England (www.thetimes.com, 2018).

Alongside the plethora of changes that have impacted on our schools in the last decade is the requirement for schools to take on responsibility for training future teachers in what are called 'teaching school alliances' in an apprentice type model of teacher training (Browne, 2017). This might offer hope for teacher supply in the future but in 2018, 20% of training places were left unfilled. This is obviously problematic for headteachers and their leadership teams. In 2018 English school headteachers took time away from their schools and, in a national show of concern and unprecedented action, marched on and through the political heartland of the United Kingdom to express their concerns.

Research by Bal and Visser (2011) based in the Netherlands suggests that as a result of pension restrictions many teachers are interested in working beyond their retirement age. The authors suggest that flexible arrangements for such members of the profession is a way of dealing with the tensions in teacher supply (Bal and Visser, 2011). They maintain that the retention of retirement-age teachers is one solution that leadership teams may wish to explore in tackling the teacher shortage problem. For the retiring teacher, however, where financial reward was not the key motivator, access to support and having a less challenging role were vital in their decision to stay in the profession and delay retirement.

It is not just at the classroom level where schools are struggling to recruit. A research project based in Oxford and intended to improve pupil achievement in 11 failing city schools (see Chapter 6) identified real pressures and problems in the recruitment and retention of headteachers. Throughout the life of the research project only one of the schools retained the same headteacher. One school experienced four changes of headteacher in two years. The following table illustrates the pressure in numerical terms as schools defined as operating 'below the floor', a measure of unacceptable pupil achievement in the school data tables (Chapter 6), struggle to interview and appoint to their leadership team. Table 11.1 illustrates the instability in the system during the life of the LfL project.

Table 11.1 Leadership changes

Only three schools (one head took maternity leave for several months, therefore requiring a different interim head) retained the same headteacher over the project period of two years. With such a fluctuating picture it is difficult to see how full commitment to and involvement in the planned intervention could be maintained and activated.

Table 11.1 Indications of changes in headteacher during the project period

Oxford City schools involved (at varied levels) in the attainment project	*Number of headteacher changes since 2012*
School A	At least 1
School B	At least 1
School C	0
School D	At least 2
School E	1
School F	At least 4
School G	At least 2
School H	0 (temporary interim)
School I	At least 1
School J	At least 3
School K	0

Source: McGregor and Browne (2015)

 ## Teacher supply issues

During the project many schools experienced several staff shortages limiting the availability of staff to attend project events which were designed to support the project ambitions. Between 2013 and 2014 one school appointed 11 new members of staff. There appeared to be a very high staff turnover in schools placed in challenging circumstances with three schools comprising an academy experiencing a turnover of 75% of staff over a summer period (Wright, 2014).

The impact of staff turbulence in many of the participating schools is reflected in the following extract, taken from the OfSTED report for School B School (www. ofstedreportrosehillschool.com).

Case study 11.1 Staff changes

School B is a larger than average primary school serving the Cowley area of Oxford with approximately 470 children on roll including 60 nursery places. Over half the children are from minority ethnic backgrounds. The number of pupils with specific needs is above average. Since the last inspection there have been major changes in staffing, a large number of the teaching staff having been appointed within the last three years. Most significant are the changes in leadership as, following a period of instability, the present headteacher has been in post since September and most members of the governing body are new. Following **a recent period of turbulence within both leadership and staffing**, the new headteacher, working in close partnership with governors, parents and children, has created within the school a warm and embracing culture.

A recent report (Weale, 2016) in the *Oxford Times* identified teacher shortages in the county. This is an issue that obviously compounds and exacerbates the challenges involved in running an effective school.

The Leadership for Learning intervention, a bespoke programme designed to support headteachers and middle leaders, offered a range of supportive activities throughout the two years. These included various lectures, seminars and workshops led by renowned, established and experienced school leaders and well-known academic researchers working in school improvement, coaching and/or leadership.

This intervention enabled school leaders to develop their confidence and competence to improve the children's attainment, increase engagement with families and develop effective collaboration with other city schools (Menter and McGregor, 2015). The successful networking between schools at different levels of leadership facilitated the sharing and dissemination of a range of effective classroom and leadership strategies to tackle some common challenges faced by the city schools.

The problems with teacher and leader supply have been exacerbated by a major reform agenda in English schools. Chapter 6 offered a list of policy changes introduced as part of national reform agenda and, as Tuytens and Devos (2014) indicate, change is never without its problems. Focusing specifically on the implementation of a teacher evaluation policy in secondary schools in Belgium it may be possible to transfer the findings and apply them to the English school system especially as the implementation of teacher evaluation forms part of the English reformed school system as a generic policy iteration for all leaders to enact. The requirement for enactment of the legislation was articulated with limited advice and guidance about implementation.

Tuytens and Devos's (2014) research identified differing perceptions of the intervention by both leaders and teachers depending on the characteristics of the leader and school. Where leaders are themselves positive about the initiative and leading a school culture that embraces change, the view of teachers tends to the same. Where the culture is less welcoming of change the policy had been disruptive and added to the tensions of leading in these environments.

Addressing the problem

Given the world shortage of teachers many leaders of education are approaching classroom teaching in different ways to keep good teachers in the profession. A number of approaches are being trialled by school leaders including flexible working alongside a strong focus on protecting the work/life balance of the school staff and the leadership team. Work/life balance (first discussed in Chapter 2) is an important issue where education systems are advanced and focused on data collection to monitor outcomes and drive improvement. It has been found that education systems focused on accountability increase the workload of teachers. In the United Kingdom, 56% of teachers reported that data collection and management caused unnecessary work. Teachers felt ill-prepared to assess student performance, analyse data and use them to inform instruction.

A study in the United States found that two-thirds of teachers lacked the facility to use data to improve instruction and often found the focus on data to be excessive (Global Education Monitoring Report, 2018). Monitoring and data collection are often seen as a necessary evil but criticised for taking time away from the 'real work' of teaching. Chapter 5 has highlighted how data has been used in the UK to drive improvements in learner outcomes. However, as illustrated in the Leadership for Learning research (Chapter 6), teachers need to understand the data and the rationale behind collecting them. Once that is understood, then, research has shown that teacher understanding leads to greater commitment and more positive outcomes (McGregor and Browne, 2015).

How can leaders keep good teachers?

Focus now turns to a specific piece of research designed to understand the factors that encourage teachers to remain working in challenging schools. While extensive research has been undertaken on the factors that cause teachers to leave their schools, there has been little focus on what encourages teachers to stay. The research, carried out by Arthur (2020), set out to explore the narratives that surround teacher retention in urban, rural and coastal schools facing severe social, economic and educational challenges. Interest in this research grew out of another research project aimed at strengthening the leadership of high-need primary schools and discussed earlier in this chapter (see also Chapter 6) where teacher retention was a key concern for the participating school leadership teams (see http://www.oxfordtimes.co.uk/news/featur es/11090715.Learning_lessons_together/), with many of the schools experiencing an annual turnover of more than 50% (Wright, 2014).

The research, entitled 'Please don't say goodbye! What makes teachers stay in challenging schools?', has identified a number of key issues that make teachers stay in the profession. The issues identified might appear as small matters but, to the teachers in the research, these are the things that made them stay in their challenging role.

The research, funded by the British Academy/Leverhulme Small Grants organisation, set out to determine the main factors that encourage teachers to stay in schools operating in challenging circumstances. The research explored a number of factors associated with teacher retention with a focus on determining the effective leadership strategies that encouraged teachers to stay.

A number of factors were identified, all of which, whether the staff were male or female, were located around issues of support, school culture, opportunities for progression and family issues, including childcare. There was also a strong thread in the data identifying the tensions and pressures impacting on teachers and leaders such as cost of living, geographic access (for example the impact the London weighting salary factor was having on recruitment to schools just outside London) and the pressures of the role.

The fragility around keeping key staff was a major concern for all headteachers with a range of strategies identified for keeping good staff. The focus was clearly on keeping those who were committed and could actually teach, rather than keeping everyone appointed to the role with one headteacher reportedly commenting: 'If you can't manage the job, please do the children a favour, just leave'.

The research revealed that the staff room culture was key to staff stability. One teacher mentioned a staff board where staff could ask for support with new ideas on ways to teach different elements of the curriculum. One staffroom had 'Prosecco Prizes', while another ran a staff reading group. The staff room was seen as the heart of the school, full of colour, humour, a place of support. Staff birthdays were celebrated in some primary schools as were staff successes.

In one secondary school, teachers commented that every meeting was focused on driving improvement. In addition, consistency in dealing with behavioural issues was considered vital. Staff reported that they wanted to be listened to and trusted. They wanted autonomy to teach the way they felt was appropriate but also required support from the leadership team when things went wrong.

Staff wanted a leader who would protect them from an onerous workload, perhaps by monitoring the number of afterschool and parents' meetings. They respected leaders who allowed staff to work from home when paperwork demands were overpowering and expected a leadership team that was resilient and aware of staff mental health.

In one primary school the headteacher said that he dealt with all parent complaints 'because that is something that can break a teacher quite quickly'. Internal promotions were seen as a way of encouraging staff to stay and one school tried to recruit pupils, on graduation, to the school-based teacher training scheme.

An open culture was considered key, one head maintaining that he was always available so that staff could 'just walk in'. The benefit of this was being able to respond to issues quickly. A secondary school head talked about involving staff in decisions, whilst also saying that sometimes he just had to 'grasp the nettle' and make difficult decisions on his own, but not before he had consulted with key staff.

From the perspective of the teachers, especially those with a young family, the existence of an onsite nursery was key, with staff being able to see their children at lunch time and be accessible quickly if their family member was ill. An understanding and flexible headteacher, preferably one who has a family and understands the pressures, was thought beneficial. The message to leaders about flexibility in recruitment and staffing was a major theme with one teacher noting that in the past the focus on an 'all or nothing approach' to working schedules and teaching posts had led to many of her colleagues leaving the profession.

An example of a leadership team protecting staff, not part of the Arthur (2020) research but relevant here, can be seen in the action taken by the leaders of The Charles Dickens School in London, the first school to retain its grade 1 status as part of the new OfSTED inspection framework first introduced in 2019 (www. ofsted.gov.uk).

Case study 11.2 The Charles Dickens School

Aware of the pressures on staff, resultant from the range of government policies introduced at speed and with minimal support, the leadership team at The Charles Dickens School asked class teachers to identify the most onerous elements of their role. The headteacher and her team wanted to discover what was putting pressure on their staff with the proviso that any suggestions made could not be core to the success of the learner. The issue raised by all staff related to time spent on marking student work, with the teachers feeling pressure to correct all mistakes and provide detailed feedback on all work. A working party was established consisting of a cross-section of staff and as a result the school marking policy was amended, reducing the expectations on staff whilst still requiring personalised feedback to support learner progress.

This approach is praised by the DfE who have noted the words of the headteacher, Cassie Buchanan, when she said: 'I have learnt that change for my teachers will only come when senior leaders take positive steps which engage with the evidence of what works for improving children's outcomes and learning from schools which are reducing workload successfully' (see https://www.gov.uk/government/news/teach er-workload-cut-by-five-hours-a-week-over-past-three-year).

Another example worthy of note can be found at Ark Conway Primary Academy in Hammersmith which has been recognised at an awards ceremony for its commitment to workplace wellbeing. The school was awarded 'Gold' in Mind's inaugural Workplace Wellbeing Index, which represents an excellent achievement for this school.

Case study 11.3 Ark Conway Primary Academy

Ark Conway's current approach to promoting mental health and wellbeing to their staff of around 30 people is built into their Mental Capital and Wellbeing Five Way Minimum offer, based on the New Economics Foundation's 'Five Ways to Wellbeing'. The school offers dedicated self-directed time at the end of each day (from 4:00 pm) so that staff can choose how to manage their own workload enabling them to schedule their work around commitments with friends and/or family, providing all staff members with a fitness tracker band and dedicated non-contact time to focus on a self-chosen area of learning.

The research and the two case studies highlight evidence of new forms of leadership in UK schools. With the increased focus on performance, leadership has been shown here to model a more collective rather than individual strategy. A new leadership paradigm is emerging with an inexorable shift away from one-way, hierarchical, organisational centric communication towards two-way, network-centric, participatory and collaborative leadership styles (McGonagill and Doefffer, 2011).

The implications of poor teacher retention for practice

Research in the US found that teacher turnover lowers student achievement, especially in lower-performing schools, and adversely affects the pupils of teachers who stay as well as those who leave (Ronfeldt et al., 2014). Possible explanations for this are that teacher turnover has a negative impact on collegiality among staff or perhaps causes a loss of institutional memory. High turnover makes planning difficult, drains financial resources and disrupts pupils' schooling (Worth et al., 2015; Darling-Hammond and Sykes, 2003).

Teacher turnover appears to be a more serious problem in schools located in areas of social and economic challenge with 'high-need' schools experiencing difficulties in attracting and keeping staff (Darling-Hammond and Sykes, 2003). A study by the UK National Audit Office (2016) found that for 54% of school leaders in socially deprived areas attracting and keeping good teachers was a major problem, compared to 33% of leaders in other schools.

Some teachers commit to staying in schools with a high proportion of children living in social and economic deprivation; however, Lynch and McCormack (2016) found no evidence that the proportion of pupils eligible for free school meals in a school influenced a teacher's intentions to leave the profession. Ronfeldt et al.

(2014:6) noted, 'A growing body of evidence indicates that more effective teachers are at least as likely, and sometimes more likely, to stay in schools than their less effective peers'. In England, the National Foundation for Educational Research (NFER) highlighted a number of 'protective' factors that appear to encourage teacher retention: 'job satisfaction, having adequate resources, reward and recognition, and being well supported by the leadership team' (Lynch and McCormack, 2016:2).

The last word on this thorny issue of teacher retention against the current backdrop of policy change and social uncertainty should perhaps come from the leaders of our schools. Projects such as the Leadership for Learning project (see Chapter 6 and earlier in this chapter) illustrate that leadership can be lonely role. The LfL research provided evidence that school leaders welcome opportunities for collegiate support from one another. The existence of collaborative partnerships and opportunities for leaders to discuss challenges is valued.

In the Oxford research one headteacher identified an internal reorganisation she implemented as being 'borrowed' from another school:

> We have been so successful with splitting the leadership teams and devolving responsibility across the school. We set up change teams and took on shared learning, and the research and the learning approach that X head had had and we put that into our school, so the assistant head for curriculum now has a termly meeting with each of the subject leaders all together as a group. Here we share data and have an open discussion about pupil learning and the strategies required to help learners and teachers reach the set goals.
>
> (Headteacher, School H)

And another head:

> The project... gave the new leadership team time to come together to discuss leadership and how we wanted to lead by example to transform a failing school. Our effective leadership has been recognised by both OfSTED and an external review.
>
> (Headteacher, School C)

Structural changes occurred in this school too:

> We want our teachers to have a positive experience of leadership, so they'll take on greater responsibility and grow in their roles. That's what we want. We want to retain staff and we want them to feel like they have a voice. We organised all teachers into leadership teams. Everybody's experiencing leadership. We allow the teams to prioritise their work, set their own challenges and their objectives and we do that in a hands-off way

and we budget time money for teachers to do that work. Then, as the head, I talk to each leadership team and ask them to talk through the performance of the team in respect of achieving the targets we have set.

(Headteacher, School C)

The comments from one headteacher demonstrate how leaders felt judged by the pressures of external data but realised they had to grapple with it. He reviewed the data in his school and compared it with other schools in the project, then used differences in achievement in these schools to identify, with his leadership team, the good practice they wanted to copy.

It's been really useful for me, meeting other heads and then going back and thinking, OK, how is School X getting 100% of conversion from Key Stage 1 to Key Stage 2, but our average children sometimes aren't doing that? So I obviously know School X is doing something that we don't know about, so we can learn from them and when I speak to other headteachers, their reading's at 90–95% possibly, where our reading – our amount of level 5s – is really high but we're not still managing to convert some children. And conversely our writing is really high compared to some other local schools, so we're doing something really right with writing but we'll need to learn from others for reading. So, that's been really, really useful. We also know that we've got some really brilliant TAs but we've just not managed them very well […] [Additionally,] to save time and capacity on the SLT, I know Schools A, B and X have already done this work, so now when we decide we want to do this we've got some models to go to and go, OK, can we use your model, and now you've implemented it can you tell us how you could have done that even better? So that we can save even more time and therefore kind of make more capacity for the future. So, it's been really, really useful and it's really good to hear that the staff have enjoyed it too.

(Headteacher, School G)

And one of the more experienced heads also suggested significant benefits:

I've really valued meeting with other headteachers and being able to talk to them and realise that some of the issues I've got are the same in other schools. That we're talking about the same issues from pupil premium to retention, being able to have that professional conversation that you can't necessarily have in your own school is important.

(Headteacher, School I)

149

And another:

> The whole culture around attainment and interpretation of the data has changed. We come together as a whole staff team and look at the data, we don't apply a blame culture and focus on specific staff (well certainly not in our team meetings), we simply identify where our learners are not making the expected progress and then we target those learners for additional support. We have open conversations and agree together where extra support is required.
>
> (Headteacher, School E, as previously mentioned)

The research interviews contained many positive comments about the opportunity provided to share data, to share examples of good practice and to work collaboratively to improve the data picture in the participating schools. Contextual analysis of all the interview data revealed no negative comments about the use of data, the national and local focus on targets or the demoralising effect of a target-driven culture on teacher performance. This lack of comment doesn't prove that negativity didn't exist, but certainly the testimony of the headteachers, as interviewed, seemed to demonstrate that data is, in alignment with Torres (2011), the new common sense in school leadership. The research revealed how the project had become a site of interconnecting practice, a place for sharing good practice and heightened ambitions for improvements in student learning (McGregor and Browne, 2015). The positive elements recorded here stand to illustrate the benefits of collaborative leadership where educationalist work together to support one another.

Collaborative leadership models acknowledge the benefits for leaders when they can move outside their own organisation to converse with others in a supportive and collegiate way. Internally, too, collaborative leadership has benefits in breaking down silos and allowing the effective sharing of good practice among colleagues on different teams.

This chapter has focused on the issue of retention and recruitment not only of teaching staff, but leaders too. It has identified some of the issues involved in maintaining a full staff complement specifically in schools operating in challenging circumstances. The role of working together in a collaborative leadership approach has given focus to how headteachers believe they can support their staff to stay in the profession whilst also revealing that leaders need a place to go too, particularly in the current times of uncertainty and challenge, to talk to one another and share their concerns. A report by the DfE assessing the impact of the educational changes required by school leaders identified the benefits of collaborative working in strong partnership associations, arguing strongly for the advancement of collaborative leadership approaches in the face of educational change (Stoll, 2015).

The competences from the National Professional Qualifications for leadership covered in this chapter are:

Analyse performance data to identify the causes of variation within a school and against comparative schools (for example, in relation to national benchmarks, historical performance or between different groups), routinely adopting a proportionate approach in the collection and use of data.

Lead, motivate and influence others, including beyond the line management chain, to deliver whole-school objectives.

Identify talent within an organisation and put in place arrangements or tools to develop and retain it.

Systematically review the cumulative impact of initiatives on teacher workload and make proportionate and pragmatic demands on staff.

References

Arthur, L. (2020) *Please don't say goodbye*. Unpublished research. Oxford: Oxford Brookes University.

Bal, M.P. and Visser, M. (2011) When are teachers motivated to work beyond retirement age? The importance of support, change of work role and money. *Journal of Educational Administration and Management*, 39 (5), 590–602.

Browne, E. (2017) *Leading a consultancy unit in a UK University*. Auckland University internal research publication for school of education research conference, 11.11.17.

Darling-Hammond, L. and Sykes, G. (2003) *A research study by the UK National Audit Office*. Norwich: Her Majesties Stationery Office.

http://www.oxfordtimes.co.uk/news/features/11090715.Learning_lessons_together

Lynch, B. and McCormack, B. (2016) Development of a model of situational leadership. *Journal of Nursing Management*, 19 (8), 1058–69.

McGonagill, G. and Doefffer, T. (2011) The leadership implications of the evolving technologies. Retrieved from http:..//www.bertelsmann-stiftung.de/cps/rde/xchg/S ID-6822B8GGFCFC3827.bst-engl/hs.xsl/1000672-101629.htmL

McGregor, D. and Browne, E. (2015) Report to Oxford City Council – leadership for learning. Available at www.oxfordcitycouncilcommitteedreport/13.2.15

Mentor, I. and McGregor, D. (2015) *Leadership for learning*. Unpublished Research. Oxford: Oxford University.

Ronfeldt, M., Owens Farmer, S. and McQueen, K. (2014) Teacher collaboration in instructional teams and student achievement. *American Educational Research Journal*, 52 (3), 234–246.

Stoll, L. (2015) *Three greats for a self-improving school system: pedagogy, professional development and leadership: executive summary (Teaching schools R&D network national themes project 2012-14)*. London: Department for Education (DfE).

Tuytens, M. and Devos, G. (2014) The problematic implementation of teacher evaluation policy: school failure or government pitfall. *Educational Management Administration and Leadership*, 42 (4), 155–174.

Torres, L. (2011) *Outstanding Leadership*. New York: The New York Leadership Academy.

UNESCO. (2018) *Accountability in education: meeting our commitments*. Global education monitoring report. Brussels: UNESCO Publications.

Weale, S. (2016) 'Criminalised' as a failing school – in the midst of Oxford's wealthy spires. Available at http://www.theguardian.com/education/2016/feb/02/failing-school-oxford-property-prices-recruit-teachers

Worth, J., Bamford, S. and Durbin, B. (2015) Should I stay or should I go? Analysis of teachers joining and leaving the profession. Slough: NFER.

Wright, A. (2014) Review of the education attainment programme including the KRM Programme. *Report presented to OCC Scrutiny Committee*, 26 September 2014.

www.thetimes:2018_exodusofteachersis alessonforpoliticians.org 26/09/18.

http://www.ofsted.gov.uk (accessed 25th May, 2020).

http://www.ofstedreportrosehillschool.com (accessed 25th May, 2020).

http://www.oxfordtimes.co.uk/news/features/1109075 (accessed 25th May, 2020).

12 | Leveraging technology

A publication from the United Kingdom government at the turn of the millennium postulated a number of models for schooling in the future. One model relied heavily on what it referred to as the new technologies for learning, with students learning online as they studied at home and attended schools, in their bodily form, less and less. This model has not materialised at the speed predicted by the DfE. However, as we experience VUCA with the impact of disease, mass displacement of people and the need to counteract decades of environmental damage, new technologies have the potential to stabilise the fragility we are experiencing and help the world establish a new equilibrium. What this means for leaders is addressed in this chapter. Rapid change towards the greater use of technology in teaching and learning is providing opportunities for new types of school leadership whilst also producing challenge. This chapter explores the use of technology as a tool for leadership and suggests the reader might assess their own readiness for a greater reliance on technology in the future whilst identifying some of the emerging challenges the new technologies pose.

Keeping abreast of change

The Open University's Institute of Educational Technology (UK) in collaboration with researchers from the National Institute for Digital Learning at Dublin City University has reported over a number of years on innovative and developing technological innovations likely to have an impact on teaching and learning. It is worth it for leaders of education to be fully aware of such innovations and their impact. Even where a distributed model (see Chapter 4) of leadership is practiced and technological experts are responsible for expenditure and renewal of technological hardware, it is important that leaders still have an understanding of the impact that new innovations might have on schooling. This aligns with models of leadership identified by Sergiovonni as pedagogic leadership (see Chapter 7).

The innovation reported in the Open University document as likely to have a major impact on teaching and learning is artificial intelligence. The term 'artificial intelligence' (AI) describes computer systems that imitate human capabilities and behaviours to allow computer interaction with real people. AI-powered learning systems are increasingly being used in educational settings with universities offering degree programmes for those interested in designing AI systems. AI has immense potential to transform education with applications such as intelligent tutoring systems, dialogue-based tutoring systems, exploratory learning environments, automatic writing evaluation and conversational agents.

One example where AI is being employed is in China where a project designed to deliver training in English using the phonics method is being designed to use AI in classrooms in a range of cities and rural areas around China. This combination of adopting the phonics method to teach English as a second language, whilst using AI to reach rural areas of China, has the potential to increase social mobility for the most disadvantaged in China. This is particularly important since the ability to pass tests in English is an essential element of graduate study in China.

The meaning of being human, and our relation to the world around us, is naturally of great importance to any conception of education. And another identified innovation, known as posthumanism, examines what it means to be human and whether being human extends beyond our bodies into the real and digital world. The being human philosophy identifies the potential that technology offers us to learn in partnership with animals and machines. For example, computer programs such as 'chatbots' that answer questions and deliver services through simulated conversations are designed to sound like humans and to evoke conversational responses from their users. This approach may have advantages if the technology is used to do good, in health care perhaps, or in dealing with basic education functions such as reporting student absences, contacting parents with standardised messages for example. However, the use of technology, when adopting a posthumanist approach to education, will require us to confront some unsettling questions about how far we are prepared to let technology take over the elements of humanity that require human interaction if we move to a position where there are less well-defined separations between humans and technology.

The ease of access to data is also considered an innovation likely to influence teaching and learning in a major way. More than 250 national, local and city governments, and a wide and growing range of global and local organisations, are now sharing the data that they create and use in their work. In Chapter 6 this text focused on the growing use of data to drive improvements in schools, with open publication of school SAT results, the preparation of national performance tables and benchmarking data to support leaders in their management of resources.

The mass collection of openly available data can also support the development of innovative learning activities with the promise of an authenticity not possible before. The data that is shared emerges from real processes occurring within organisations. It is often data that is used in professional work that has a real impact on our lives and the world around us. This data can have personal relevance to our learners offering the potential for a motivated engagement at the local, national or international level. Learners can also identify issues that require attention locally or across wider society. In one example primary school students can compare school timetables with time spent on different subjects across their country and further afield. Engagement with open data connects learners with encouragement towards data literacy, transparency and evidence-based action.

The growing use of digital technologies in educational contexts is accompanied by an ever-increasing range of ethical questions such that ethical data management becomes another area of interest. There are the many ethical issues centred on data, such as who owns the data, how the data should be interpreted and how the privacy of learners and teachers should be protected. Leaders of education will be aware of the data protection legislation in the UK which makes the protection of private information about learners and staff a central role in the leadership of schools. It is important for those in a leadership role to be aware of the legal position around data collection and sharing and to ensure that all staff are compliant with the legislation.

There is increased pressure on educational institutions to start to develop policies relating to data ethics, to obtain consent from students to use and analyse any data from their interactions with their learning management system and to provide effective training and support for students and staff. Students need to understand how their data might be used and the possible consequences. When preparing learners for a changing world, teachers might enable learners to 'play' with their own data and learn what the limitations of sharing it may be. Engaging with data ethics is part of how institutions are developing effective learning cultures in a digital world.

The issue of the controlled use of technologies such as mobile phones in the classroom is best addressed with a focus on what is referred to as 'social justice pedagogy'. Most people want to be fair and just towards others, but sometimes it is difficult to do this in practice as our unconscious biases can get in the way. Education has a role to play in helping learners to address their unconscious biases as well as the injustices in their own lives and in society. Social justice pedagogy aims to educate and enable students to become active citizens who understand social inequalities and can contribute to making society more democratic and egalitarian. To achieve this, systems of power, dominance, privilege or oppression may be critically explored with students. The school leadership team may wish to encourage learners to engage with processes of activism such as protests as in the case of coordinated protests against abuse of the environment with young people taking time off school to express their concerns at a global level. Leaders of education will want to facilitate an open discussion around themes of social justice and encourage appropriate forms of protest that will have a positive impact.

Social justice pedagogy involves elements of student voice and empowerment emphasising the importance of involving and engaging students in building the curriculum rather than having a curriculum imposed on them. It may also involve paying attention to how sub-cultures, marginalised groups or under-represented people are portrayed in published learning materials and in the wider context of local and global media. Later in this chapter a research project is described which identified the involvement of learns in making decisions about technology, as an example of social justice pedagogy.

Another area where technology is having an impact is in competitive video gaming known as esports which involves sport played on the internet, individually or in teams. Esports have become a global leisure activity, but they also offer opportunities for education. They illustrate a way to reach young people and connect them to virtual sporting activities. This might induce learners to partake in sports themselves. Variations of esports have been used in school subjects such as physical education to support students' understanding of movement and of different rules or techniques in sports and games, and as a teaching aid. They can also be a way to support digital literacy, numeracy, socialisation and teamwork. For example, data from esports games could be analysed by the participants to suggest team strategies to improve performance. A well-known esports platform, Twitch, enables recording of group activity, interaction between teachers and learners and opportunities for amateur online instruction among peers. A project designed by two sports coaches from Oxfordshire, entitled visual ideas (www.visualideas.com), encourages challenges in sport with homework tasks set for parents and students to complete together.

Some topics are hard to teach, for example explaining how the heart pumps blood, and here learning through animation is coming to the fore. Students can be shown short animated movies of a dynamic process. Animations can show how an expert tackles a difficult problem, such as solving a complex equation. They can also show abstractions from the real world, such as the growth of a city. These are useful in stimulating interest and promoting engagement. Learners with special educational needs can benefit from animations that explain an important idea clearly and succinctly, such as how to stay safe online. Learner-created animations are also a way to support self-expression and have been used as prompts for creative activities such as story writing. Some early research studies showed that animations were no better than textbook pictures, but recent research has focused on the conditions that make animations successful as tools for learning (Kukulska-Hulme et al., 2020). Studies have shown that animations can be better than pictures when they are well-designed, are based on sound principles and teach processes or skills, and when students are in control. In primary schools today programmes using animation are introduced to teach concepts such as shapes, numbers, counting and other mathematical concepts.

Listening to a teacher and using our eyes, along with visual approaches such as looking at books and watching videos, used to be the central means of perception for learning. This model ignores the fact that we have many senses, including touch, taste and smell. This has led to the use of multisensory experiences, in which several senses are stimulated. Museums wishing to capture a real-life experience, such as the underground Saxon Village in York, add the sense of smell to the experience so that participants can better experience what it was like to live in Saxon times. Researchers at the Open University (www.innovativepedagogy.ou.ac.uk) believe that education and training delivery in the future will be multisensory. All the senses are currently receiving more attention in education, due to advancements in technology. Evidence shows that stimulation of sensory channels and combinations of channels during learning can prove beneficial, resulting in learning gains and deeper understanding, as well as greater enjoyment. Multisensory teaching and learning can enhance communication, engagement, memorisation and understanding. Again, it can be extremely powerful for students with learning difficulties whose difficulties might be caused by limited functionality in one or more areas of the senses.

Networked learning via digital networks is a widely adopted pedagogical approach since it promotes connections among learners, teachers, communities and resources. This might include setting up online network groups for planned research projects, such as those designed in reusable learning objects (RLOs) that involve learners bringing together evidence they have researched to complete a project (Browne, 2008). It might also involve the use of flipped learning, a teaching methodology that requires learners to research a topic prior to its being launched in school, with learners presenting what they have been directed to access on the network, and the teacher posing questions and drawing the topic together.

Enabling users to harness the power of technological devices and take advantage of networked learning without the internet has been made possible by low cost, low power network hubs like Raspberry Pie. This approach is called offline networked learning; it can support conversation, collaboration, resource sharing, visualisation and consolidation, thus enhancing the process of learning as well as the outcomes. For example, the approach has been used in rural Zambia to enable teachers to come together from different village schools to access digital teaching resources, share their own materials with other teachers during training workshops and take selected materials back to their own schools (www.innovativepedagogy.ou.ac.uk).

In the science disciplines we are seeing the use of online laboratories which enable students to apply their knowledge and develop their skills. An online laboratory is an interactive environment for creating and conducting simulated science experiments. The lab could be accessed through the web or as a programme running on a computer, either in the classroom or at home. The aim is for a student to experience the procedures of carrying out a science experiment, including the consequences of making mistakes, and to get results. Online labs can also allow students to interact with real scientific equipment in 'remote labs'. Despite concerns that some aspects of practical work such as the sights and smells of experiments in the physical laboratory are missing from the experience, virtual labs are becoming mainstream in higher education for science and engineering in many countries around the world (Kukulska-Hume et al., 2020).

The overarching impact of the technologies identified is that education will become much more based on experience. The owner of Facebook Mark Zuckerberg has understood this very well: 'Education is on the cusp of a technology revolution that will transform teaching and learning to an experience-based approach'.

As a result, Facebook are working on creating more immersive hardware, tools and experiences focusing on augmented and virtual reality as the next step in the evolution of computer-based instruction. Facebook see the new technologies as redefining the way we teach and learn, transforming education and turning classrooms into 21st-century technologically advanced places of learning. And to emphasise the power of these technologies, Facebook maintain that technology and content will not only increase engagement and knowledge retention, but will also provide access to education regardless of distance and help students become innovative creators (www.facebook.org.futureplanning).

During the global pandemic of 2020 families kept in touch using a range of technological innovations as did schools in an attempt to cover the curriculum when schools were closed for an extensive period of time. The software adopted included:

- Google drive, with the option to collaborate on the production of documents.
- Zoom, as a source for video conferencing.
- Slack/Gitter with free instant messaging.
- Skype, also free with access for two people at a time.
- WhatsApp, which allows up to four people to communicate simultaneously by speech and video.
- Microsoft Teams, which is multifunctional and allows video conferencing. This system was used by many schools in the UK during the global pandemic of 2020 with teachers setting up individual classrooms and posting work for their classes to complete whilst on lockdown.

The role that technology can play in supporting the delivery of teaching and learning was starkly and swiftly realised when schools across the world had to be closed in 2020. Measures as extreme as closing schools can be socially disruptive and tend to burden vulnerable populations and most specifically if families don't have access to technology and cannot stay in touch through virtual means. One of the terminal problems associated with the use of technology for learning will be maintaining access for all irrespective of geographic access and the ability to purchase the required resources.

 ## Are school leaders ready to embrace change?

Leaders in the future will have to be innovative. They will need to embrace technology and be aware of the power it has to enable people to teach and learn in ways never thought possible before. With the ability to share quality content, along with virtual collaboration and student creation, we are moving to an immersive model of education and making learning more personal, powerful and connected to the real world. Leaders of education will have to stay abreast of technological advances if they are to maintain their credibility in our fastmoving world.

 ## The student voice on technology

When discussing the emerging models of technological change, mention was made of needing to take into account the views of learners. Researchers have referred to natives and immigrants (Prensky, 2001) in describing the young and more mature in their approaches to technology. The youth of today are growing up using technology as part of their learning experience whereas those in leadership positions may not be universally as competent in its use nor aware of all new developments. This has implications for leaders of education. Aware of the challenges, JISC (the Joint Information Systems Committee) commissioned a study on the views of students in higher education entitled 'Investigating students' expectations of the digital environment' (www.digitalstudents. jiscinvolve.org). The research was designed to discover how developments in mobile technology, web and social media trends, and the widespread use of technology in schools were impacting on the expectations of students arriving into higher education. The research was extended to include a study of the students in the FE and skills sectors. This research, as a counter to the rhetoric of 'student as consumer', embraced the student engagement agenda and tried to articulate the relational metaphors that characterise the developing relationships between students and staff in the area of technology. The research, interested in how organisations have been developing strategies to give focus to student voice, identified a staged approach with the following categories identified:

- Inform, where learners are informed about their rights and ways in which to participate in the organisation.
- Consult, where organisations seek the views of learners and provide feedback on any decisions taken.

159

- Involve, where staff and learners work closely together to make sure all views are understood and notice is taken.
- Collaborate, where aspects of decision-making involve a partnership with learners.
- Empower, where learners control their own learning, set agendas for change and contribute to management decisions.

(LSIS/nus 2013:7)

The JISC research project resulted in a further level of engagement proposed by Browne and Miller (2018) with the category of active engagement added to the list where institutions are empowering students to be actively involved in technological developments and decision-making. One college, identified by Browne and Miller, had appointed students to the role of 'Digi-Pals', trained by e-learning staff and given the job of enriching cross-college digital practice.

The first innovative approach noted in the case study institution was one of structural organisation. The head of e-learning was appointed to a merged department bringing together technology specialists, learning technologists, teachers and students. The merging of academic and technical staff as an action of deliberative excellence (Tettegah et al., 2006) created a culture shift with the embedding of high-quality technological expertise into everyday teaching practice. Prior to structural reorganisation the college had relied on appointing subject-based e-learning champions as promoted by the Learning and Skills Improvement Service (www.LSISe-cpd). The next innovative step was to abolish this role and reallocate four e-learning champions to a cross-institutional Digi-Pal post working with six student Digi-Pals who had to undergo a rigorous interview process before being appointed.

The selection of the appointed Digi-Pals had mirrored that of an employment exercise with an internal advert posted around the college and on the institutional intra-net, application required in writing by a set date, formal interviews and letter of appointment to the selected appointees. This resulted in eight applicants with six appointments made. The two students who were not appointed were offered advice and guidance as how to improve their application should another round of appointments be made during their period of study at the college.

The successfully appointed student Digi-Pals were given identifying 'hoodies' to wear, allocated funds of £1,100 each for carrying out their new role and given an iPad. Quasi-employment as a Digi-Pal involved the students signing a contract with expectations of regular attendance at staff meetings. The Digi team met regularly and three missed meetings would result in a loss of role. The Digi-Pals have been actively involved in enriching the digital activities of the institution by producing safety videos, creating an 'App of the Month' communication and engaging in learning walks around the college offering support to learners and staff. The students are part of the college e-learning department and are consulted on all matters digital. The research revealed that the Digi-Pals felt their role to be significant, their voice to be heard and their contribution valued. In the interviews the Digi-Pals talked about their active contribution to decision-making in the e-learning departmental meetings and described their role as empowering, as a partnership with staff that was truly collaborative.

By becoming additional technological support in the organisation, the Digi-Pals were trained in the use of assistive software to support other students and staff in the use of learning enhancing technologies. These include a 'Jaws' package for the visual impaired, screen magnifying equipment, Dragon Naturally speaking software which changes speech into text, Braille software, Claro software which will read scanned elements of text in speech form and an Omni page which can translate and reformulate documents. In addition, Digi-Pals have engaged in film-making and editing, and supported staff and students in the use of presentational tools such as Prezi (for more information on these resources please see www.blackburn.ac.uk).

Using funding from a 'Learning Futures' initiative the team of Digi-Pals designed a continuing professional development (CPD) programme on the use of technology for learning. In designing the programme, 'the Digi-Pals collaborated internally and externally and bridged the gap between teachers, learners and technical teams' (http:/learmingfutures.com). The Digi-Pals actively engaged in creating new resources for learning becoming active agents in promoting the digital agenda in the college.

What does this mean for leadership?

Encouraging the active engagement of students in decision-making is a developing part of new emerging models of leadership. This is a leadership approach which accepts the greater knowledge and enthusiasms of younger staff and students. And as far as engagement with technology is concerned the role of the leader is one of 'sense making' in a rapidly changing world. In addition, leaders will need to be prepare to accept that they don't know everything and be prepared as a result to acknowledge the knowledge of others and work collaboratively.

Online schools for children with learning difficulties

There are already in existence schools which deliver the curriculum online known as virtual schools. These tend to be private schools designed to support learners with learning difficulties but there are such schools run by local authorities as well. Case study 12.1 exemplifies an online school operating in the UK. The extract is taken from the school website.

> **Case study 12.1 InterHigh**
>
> The UK's leading online school
>
> Established in 2005, InterHigh is a complete interactive Primary School, Secondary School and Sixth Form College. We welcome pupils from across the UK and Internationally. Rather than travelling to school to study – InterHigh comes to you, wherever you are, through our specialised learning portal. We are able to offer you everything you expect from a traditional school… plus a whole lot more!
>
> Our entire online curriculum is taught by our expert, experienced staff whose passion for their subject is matched by their motivation and energy to see every pupil succeed. Once lessons are over, pupils can enjoy a range of clubs, societies, seminars or catch up with friends in the common room or on the school's own social platforms.

A report from the English Department for Education entitled 'Realising the Potential of Technology in Education' (DfE, 2019) identifies developing good practice in all education sectors. It records specifically that:

> At Woodberry Down Primary School in London teachers use cloud technology to share resources and collaborate, saving themselves hours of time a week. Grimsby Institute of Further and Higher Education uses virtual and augmented reality to better prepare students for vocational careers. Nottingham Trent University is using data to help understand their students' engagement with their chosen degrees, allowing tutors to target interventions to better support their students.
>
> (DfE, 2019:2)

The DfE report suggests that:

> Technology works best in education when strategically introduced by skilled and confident staff. The best leaders place a strong focus on how technology can improve processes and teaching, they build digital capability amongst their staff and achieve good value for money through their procurement. We know however that many leaders can struggle to know where to start with technology; they may be experts in education but are often not experts in digital technology.
>
> (DfE, 2019:24)

In order to assess where you are in terms of progressing with the use of technology in your organisation use Table 12.1 to assess your readiness for the technological challenges ahead.

Task 12.1 Review the grid

EVOLUTIONARY		TRANSITIONAL	REVOLUTIONARY	
1 LOCALISED	2 CO-ORDINATED	3 TRANSFORMATIVE	4 EMBEDDED	5 INNOVATIVE Key note: Demand-led, customer-focused provision
Responsibility for IT delegated to identified staff.	A co-ordinated approach to IT development encouraged and supported.	Staff encouraged to use confidently a wide range of IT. Staffing structure reviewed and appropriate new posts created and supported by senior management.	Ensures that IT is used across the curriculum and administrative applications.	Strategic commitment to IT in learning.
Takes place mainly in isolation with little co-ordination of IT across the institution.	Central IT management function identified. Involved in curriculum development to co-ordinate IT practice across the institution. Contributes to planning of staff development.	Acts as a catalyst for change. Takes account of current applications of IT in education. Supports the development of differentiated learning programmes through IT.	Monitors and supports IT integration across the curriculum. Is able to advise on models of good practice and innovation.	
Learning resources are managed without reference to IT resources.	Senior member of staff has overall responsibility for all learning resources. Learning resource and IT management are co-ordinated.	Learning and IT resource provision co-ordinated and integrated.	Learning resources are available in a range of formats and locations to provide support for a range of needs.	
Policy not developed but some staff, or departments, are integrating IT in their schemes of work.	Draft IT policy in place which bears reference to the overarching college mission. Extent of IT use identified and recorded. Full inventory of resources available.	Staff actively contribute to the process of updating and expanding existing IT policy and to its implementation in the curriculum.	IT policy takes account of changes in teaching and learning styles arising from the potential of its exploitation.	

Staff development	Individual training for personal development is provided on an ad-hoc basis.	A co-ordinated approach to generic IT training e.g. spreadsheets, word processing, databases. Recognition of additional skills to support the integration of IT in the curriculum.	Curriculum- and MIS-based IT training for most staff by internal and external trainers. Appropriate training for non-teaching staff. Recognition of new skills needed to facilitate changing teaching and learning styles.	IT is integrated intuitively into all areas of the work of the college. Staff take responsibility for identifying their own staff development needs.	Staff trained in tutoring and timely intervention. *(DEVELOPMENT)*
Integration of curriculum and administration data	Limited IT use in curriculum and in administration. MIS used for administration.	Staff recognise the value of IT in handling administration and curriculum data.	Outputs used to support planning and decision making.	Staff systematically use IT systems to generate curriculum and management information.	Flexible course delivery using IT appropriately. *(ADMINISTRATION)*
Teaching and learning styles	Individual lecturers and students explore the potential of IT in learning in an ad-hoc way.	IT used to support and enhance existing teaching and learning practice across the institution.	New, IT-based approaches to teaching, supporting a range of learning styles, incorporated into curriculum planning, policy and practice.	Lecturers recognise its power to encourage higher order skills, e.g. problem solving. Suitable uses of IT incorporated into learning strategies.	
Student IT skills	Some staff exploit students' basic IT skills but with little attempt to integrate IT into learning and assessment process.	Curriculum areas provide contexts for the development of IT skills and their assessment. Generic skills may be developed through IT courses.	Staff acknowledge high level of student IT skills and devise appropriate learning situations which reflect and allow development of those skills.	Student use of IT skills is appropriate in the context of their learning experiences and its application is regularly re-evaluated.	

					LINKS
Technical support	Technical support sporadic and unreliable. No systematic procedures in place.	Centrally managed and co-ordinated technical support. Support request, fault reporting, etc. procedures clearly defined.	Non-academic support staff available to support student learning and staff development activities.	Technical and learning support roles have evolved to encompass developmental and advisory activities.	Efficient, customer-driven resource deployment.
Funding	IT is funded on an ad-hoc basis.	IT is funded to reflect priorities identified in a strategic plan. Centrally co-ordinated funding of IT through a single budget holder.	Funding recognises role of IT in developing teaching and learning strategies. Staff development represents a significant proportion of overall IT funding programme.	Innovative methods of funding IT developments are explored and exploited.	
Physical resources	Individual department control and explore potential of IT resources.	Provision of IT facilities is centrally funded and co-ordinated. Provision recognises the importance of non-curriculum-specific applications of IT in the learning process.	A mixed economy of provision leading to resource areas being developed throughout the institution, e.g. IT in science or art and design areas.	Open access to IT resources which are increasingly used for flexible and independent learning.	
External links	Informal links developed by individual departments that exploit IT resources and/or expertise of commercial, industrial, academic and other institutions.	The institution's links with external agencies centrally co-ordinated. Links regularly reviewed and considered for mutual benefit.	Impact of external links on curriculum focus. The community and other external agencies provide support, e.g. local employers contribute to curriculum review and development.	Contact with the external agencies influences the development of the institution's thinking on the educational use of IT.	Focus on community improvement through education.

				DEVELOPMENT
Record keeping	Individuals or departments use IT for simple record-keeping e.g. word-processed student lists or simple databases.	A co-ordinated and central-ised approach to record-keeping is implemented across the institution. Data entered mainly by administrative staff.	Individual lecturers actively engage with a centralised MIS. Some academic staff access the system online.	Data entry and retrieval is an accepted part of every lecturer's practice.	Diagnostic assessment and guidance on demand.
Evaluation and assessment	Reacts to external pressure, e.g. GNVQ.	College looks outward (e.g. to other institutions) for examples of good practice.	Systematic use of IT for assessment, recording and reporting.	IT-based record systems used to inform curriculum development and planning in the institution.	
Staff development	Individual training for personal development is provided on an ad-hoc basis.	A co-ordinated approach to generic IT training e.g. spreadsheets, word processing, databases. Recognition of additional skills to support the integration of IT in the curriculum.	Curriculum- and MIS-based IT training for most staff by internal and external trainers. Appropriate training for non-teaching staff. Recognition of new skills needed to facilitate changing teaching and learning styles.	IT is integrated intuitively into all areas of the work of the college. Staff take responsibility for identifying their own staff development needs.	Staff trained in tutoring and timely intervention.

Task 12.2 Evaluate your organisation

After completing the grid, critically evaluate your organisation's preparedness for the digital future proposed in the DfE (2019) report.

Leadership approach

A range of different leadership styles will be required to address the expectations of the DfE (2019) report for the increased use of technology, not least the ability to inspire others to change and adapt. Some teachers will need convincing that using technology can reduce their workload (as suggested in the government report) as well as help with some of the challenges they face. This will demand an inspirational approach to leadership.

Inspirational leadership, at its core, is about finding ways to enhance the potential of those you lead in a way that works for them, and inspiring others to push themselves, achieve more and reach that potential. The methods by which this is done will vary from person to person, and business to business, but the outcome is always the same – people developing a greater confidence in what they can do, and applying this confidence in a way that benefits the organisation they work for (www.underscore.co).

Here, where leadership might strive to inspire others it is important to have an open mind and open approach, willing to accept small steps towards change which within the philosophy of atomic leadership can have large-scale impact.

Small accomplishments are important, as they can boost inspiration, setting off a productive and creative cycle. Dess and Picken (2000) argue that 'our competitive global economy requires leaders to shift their focus from efficient management to effective utilization of […] resources'.

They identify five key roles of leadership:

1. Using strategic vision to motivate and inspire.
2. Empowering employees at all levels.
3. Accumulating and sharing internal knowledge.
4. Gathering and integrating external information.
5. Challenging the status quo and enabling creativity. (Dess and Picken, 2000:34)

The role of leadership may well be enhanced by use of technology but there will be challenges for leaders to navigate, not least being able to stay in touch with the rapid developments that are part and parcel of our technologically advancing world.

The competences from the National Professional Qualifications for Leadership covered in this chapter are:

Deploy staff, financial, estate and educational resources within a team efficiently, to enhance pupil progress and attainment.

Recognise their strengths and weaknesses and identify learning linked to their needs.

Use appropriate tools to identify your own and staff development needs.

Lead a successful whole-school change programme.

Be an inspiring leader in a range of different situations.

Communicate and negotiate with different people effectively to make progress on objectives.

References

Browne, E. (2008) *Preparing the teach in the learning and skills sector.* London: Pearsons.

Browne, E. and Millar, D. (2018) Increasing student voice and empowerment through technology: not just listening to the voice of the learner but using their digital capabilities to benefit a whole college community. *Journal of Further and Higher Education*, 43 (10), 1433–1443.

Department for Education. (2019) *Realising the potential of technology in education.* Norwich: Her Majesties Stationery Office.

Dess, G. and Picken, J. (2000) Changing roles: leadership in the 21st century. *Journal of Organizational Dynamics*, 2 (4), 230–239.

Kukulska-Hulme, A., Beirne, E., Conole, G., Costello, E., Coughlan, T., Ferguson, R., FitzGerald, E., Gaved, M., Herodotou, C., Holmes, W., Mac Lochlainn, C., Nic Giolla Mhichíl, M., Rienties, B., Sargent, J., Scanlon, E., Sharples, M. and Whitelock, D. (2020) *Innovating pedagogy 2020: Open University innovation report 8.* Milton Keynes: The Open University.

Prensky, M. (2001) Digital natives, digital immigrants. *MCB University Press*, 9 (5), 231–255.

Tettegah, S., Kona, T. and Won Whang, E. (2006) Can virtual reality simulations be used as a research tool to study empathy, problems solving and perspective taking of educators: theory, method and application. *University of Illinois at Urbana-Champaign educators programme*, July 2006 pages 35–41.

www.digitalstudents.jiscinvolve.org (accessed 20th May, 2020).

www.facebook.org.futureplanning (accessed 20th May, 2020).

www.LSISe-cpd (accessed 15th June, 2010).

www.undescore.org.uk (accessed 20th May, 2020).

www.visualideas.com (accessed 20th May, 2020).

13 | Managing resources and risk

Reference has been made throughout this text to the volatile nature of our current existence. The situation is no less pressing in matters associated with finance and economics where the pillars of capitalism and the ideology of the free market are being challenged (Mazzucato, 2018). Financial tensions pervade the arrangements for schooling across the world with governments failing to factor in education as a value product that enhances society. In the words attributed to Oscar Wilde we seem to know 'the price of everything and the value of nothing'. This problem is apparent in the UK system where school leaders are returning deficit budgets on an annual basis as school funding fails to address raising demands. Primarily the focus here is on the challenges facing governments across the world trying to fund policy ambitions for increased access and improved quality education.

Reference was made in the introduction to this chapter to the work of Mazzucato (2018) and her book *The Value of Everything*. She builds on the central argument of her earlier work, *The Entrepreneurial State*, and argues that we undervalue the role that governments play in creating value. She maintains that the state has played an important part in innovation in the modern economy. The state, argues Mazzucato, has been instrumental in the creation of some of the technologies that underpin the biggest companies in the world – the US Department of Defence, for example, was behind both the GPS that Uber relies on and the plumbing that made Google's search algorithms possible.

In her latest book, Mazzucato argues that value-extractors (e.g. big technical, big pharmaceuticals and big finance) are rewarded more highly than value-creators (e.g. state research agencies) in modern capitalist society. By mistaking the former for the latter, Western societies are becoming increasingly unequal, and are failing to achieve sustainable growth. She points out that value, today, is understood as anything that can reach a price in the market; as a result, price determines value – a principle that is exploited by capitalists in various sectors who can become very rich very quickly without providing any benefit for society.

For stability and security in the modern world it is important to reignite a debate that was once central to economics and ask what is value, why does it matter, and who creates it? In posing such questions and giving greater value to a quality educational experience for all, we may be able to reduce the pressures that are creating instability and uncertainty in our world today.

An international perspective

For many decades now world leaders have attempted to give universal education a high priority. The Universal Declaration of Human Rights as published in 1948 first established the right for every child to receive free education. Article 26 clearly states:

> Everyone has the right to education. Education shall be free, at least in the elementary and fundamental stages. Elementary education shall be compulsory. Technical and professional education shall be made generally available and higher education shall be equally accessible to all on the basis of merit.
>
> (United Nations, https://www.un.org/en/universal-declaration-human-rights)

In the same spirit, representatives of countries from around the world came together in 2015 to agree on ten Sustainable Development Goals (SDGs) (see Chapter 11). Here, the focus is on the ambition for secondary education. The goal agreed for education is that by 2030 'all young people should be completing secondary school of good quality'
(https://www.un.org/sustainabledevelopment/sustainable-development-goals).

For this to be achieved much has to change. Between 2010 and 2015, on average, only 45% of young people were completing secondary school.

The only way forward is for more and better financing if the SDG ambition is to be achieved. However, taking into account COVID 19, the funding gap in poorer countries risks increasing to US$ 200 billion annually if action is not taken. At the time of writing, the global ambitions of the SDG appear to be unachievable with many developing countries not having the appropriate finances necessary to create schools, provide schooling materials or appoint qualified teachers. Funds pledged by the international community are generally not sufficient enough to allow countries to establish an education system for all children. Further, natural disasters in some parts of the developing and developed world create additional pressure. Even where investment has been forthcoming, it is rarely enough, resulting in poorly trained teachers and limited resources for effective pedagogic outcomes.

The right to education worldwide

As a result of poverty and marginalisation, more than 72 million children around the world remain unschooled. Sub-Saharan Africa is the most affected area with over 32 million children of primary school age remaining uneducated. Central and eastern Asia, as well as the Pacific, are also severely affected by this problem with more than 27 million uneducated children. Additionally, these regions must desire to solve continuing problems of educational poverty (defined as a child in education for fewer than four years) and extreme educational poverty (a child in education for fewer than two years).

The lack of schooling and poor education has negative effects on the population and country. The children leave school without having acquired the basics, which greatly impedes the social and economic development of these countries. The challenges for politicians, regional and district educational leaders and school leaders are large and require specific forms of resilience, determination and fortitude.

A call for political leadership

The issue of political leadership, and the desire to appoint leaders who command legitimacy, is problematic and critical in developing nations. Boutros Boutros-Ghali, a former Secretary General of the United Nations, argues that leadership in the developing world cannot be visualised within the context of individuals and their decision to act in moments of conflict. He identified the following features as conducive to leadership in emerging countries: 1) vision; 2) eloquence; 3) cooperative spirit; 4) courage; and 5) political intuition (speech to the United Nations Assembly, 1995). In general, having a clear vision suggests that in order for a leader to lead effectively they must comprehend the nature of the society in which the leadership role is to be performed. Thus, in order to construct a society that advances democracy, development and human rights, for example, a leader must be able to articulate such a vision with eloquence, working in a cooperative spirit with the immediate elite and followers. This supposition is fundamentally significant because leadership in underdeveloped communities cannot be demonstrated in a vacuum. It also requires courage and political intuition as a leader may have to, from time to time, make decisions that work against corporate and elite interests in order to maximise the efficiency of the system as a whole (Udogu, 2007).

171

Modalities and instrumentalities for effective political leadership

Effective political leadership on a global scale requires governments of nation-states to perform effectively for their citizens. Effective political leadership delivers high security for the state and the person; a functioning rule of law; education; health; and a framework conducive to economic growth. It requires the development of effective arteries for commerce and the protection of personal and human freedoms. Crucially, good political leaders provide their citizens with a sense of belonging to a national enterprise of which everyone can be proud. They knit rather than unravel their nations and seek to be remembered for how they have bettered the real lives of the governed rather than the fortunes of the few.

Given the fragility of world structures and the ambiguity surrounding political stability in some regions, strong political leadership, aligned to the desire to improve education outcomes, is key to world stability and economic development.

India's solution to financing education

Despite evidence of increased global engagement, India is still one of the countries that faces education challenges. More than half of children are unable to read and understand a simple text by the age of ten, and disparities in learning levels persist between states and between the poorest and wealthiest children (Wright-Gustafsson, 2019). However, in recent years there has been an interest in testing new financial solutions. India is playing a leading role in the use of innovative financing for development. One such innovative tool is an impact bond, a type of outcome-based financing structure where upfront capital is given to service providers by investors. While evidence on outcome-based financing in education – and impact bonds specifically – is still emerging, there are key lessons to be drawn for the application of such tools to education in India.

Focus is given here to two applications of impact bonds in the field of education. The first is the Educate Girls development impact bond (DIB), where the UBS Optimus Foundation provided upfront capital with the investment repaid by the Children's Investment Fund Foundation (CIFF) after three years. The second model, focused on strengthening literacy and numeracy across the spectrum, also in India, was funded by the UBS Optimum Foundation; if metrics are successfully achieved, the Michael and Susan Dell Foundation, together with a group of outcome funders convened by the British Asian Trust, will pay for the outcomes.

For outcome-based investments to work, impact bonds require clearly articulated intended outcomes. In the case of Educate Girls DIB these are to improve levels of Hindu and English for girls in grades 3 to 5. The Educate Girls DIB had a project budget of USD $270,000. It reached 7,300 children, covering 166 schools across 140 villages in Bhilwara, Rajasthan and had an 80% focus on achieving learning gains and a 20% focus on achieving enrolment of girls. The DIB model applied what is defined as a blended finance approach where 'start-up' or what has been called 'catalytic' capital from public or philanthropic sources is used to increase private sector investment in sustainable development. The Educate Girls DIB reported a return on capital investment for those who provided upfront capital whilst also recording major improvements in the areas set out as objectives when the DIB was first proposed. After only three years, the DIB had overachieved its enrolment and learning targets, and the investment was repaid by the CIFF.

The second project in education, the Quality Education India (QEI) DIB, brings together four service providers – Gyan Shala, Kaivalya Education Foundation, the Society for All Round Development and Educational Initiatives (Mindspark)/Pratham Infotech Foundation – to implement a range of interventions with the goal of improving learning outcomes over a four-year period through to 2022. It is too early to draw any conclusions as to the impact of this particular DIB and it is impossible to determine how global uncertainty and worldwide financial upheaval will impact the success of this venture. Only time will tell.

The potential of impact bonds

For stakeholders interested in using impact bonds to solve education challenges in India, the evidence suggests that the motivation for using the tool should be carefully considered. For instance, impact bonds seem to be most suitable to services that are preventative in nature, have a strong need for adaptation to individual needs and result in easily measured but meaningful outcomes.

Thus far globally, impact bonds have focused on building quality in existing education systems and targeting services to specific groups, rather than being used broadly for the provision of basic education. This is partly a reflection of the early stage of the impact bond market: Many existing deals have focused on testing the model and building knowledge. However, it also suggests that the most appropriate programs for impact bond financing are not experimental programs without an evidence base (since these will likely be unappealing to investors) nor well-established programs with demonstrated outcomes (since outcome funders may just want to pay for these outright). Rather, they are something in between, where there is enough risk or capacity-building needed to justify the engagement and repayment of investors. Ensuring that interventions effectively target the population in need is a crucial element of the design phase, and further research will be needed to understand the costs and benefits of the tool (Wright-Gustafsson, 2019).

More local finance arrangements

Another example used to support education social enterprise is impact loans, where the interest rate fluctuates based on the outcomes achieved. The interest on the loan is set up to be repaid on a sliding scale which decreases as learning outcomes increase. This operates rather like a model being discussed post-COVID-19 to support students to afford tuition fees for higher education. This is referred to as a student income sharing agreement (ISA). This model allows graduates, once they start working and earning above the minimum income threshold, to make income-based repayments for their loans (Wright- Gustafsson, 2019).

Does the impact bond model have potential?

The use of impact bonds to fund education is new and innovative. A proof of concept has been developed and the model reviewed and tested. The evidence offered earlier suggests the emergence of an innovative approach to funding but more research is needed to confirm the integrity of the approach. Further, critics may well see this as the marketisation of education on a grand scale. However, given the flux underway in the global environment, numerous new approaches will be required.

The leadership of financial matters in the UK context

For the United Kingdom and specifically for schools in England, financial pressures dominate the considerations of school leadership teams. With the introduction of local management of schools, a reduction in local authority influence particularly in academy provision and the focus on individual school leadership responsibility for budgets, support with financial matters has become crucial for the effective operation of schools. Indeed, the financial stability of a school is one consideration in the OfSTED inspection framework with data on school spending published on the Department for Education (DfE) website and readily available for general interrogation. A number of schools are currently reporting a deficit budget in the hope, one can only postulate, of 'surviving' until increased funding support, as promised in budget declarations, comes to fruition.

School funding allocations are made on the basis of a set amount per pupil with additional funding known as a 'pupil premium' available for pupils with designated special educational requirements. More money is allocated for pupils aged 11 and above when educated in the secondary system than to those in primary schooling.

Given the standardisation of basic income received it is perceived possible that comparisons can be made between schools across the country. This in theory should allow leadership teams to compare their expenditure with that of schools of similar size and income. This is facilitated through what is known as a benchmarking tool (www.dfes.benchmarking). This is presented as a resource to help school leaders run their institutions with the budget available and is advertised as enabling leaders to:

- View your school's financial data.
- See how similar schools manage their finances.
- Use the information gathered to establish relationships with other schools.

(www.dfes.becnhmarking)

The intention is that leaders will plan their budgets more effectively and efficiently and have the confidence to make the changes required to ensure their school runs within the available budget.

Task 13.1 Financial benchmarking

If you access this text from outside the UK then you may wish to explore what sort of support is available to those managing education budgets in your country. You may wish to visit the DfE website used in the UK to see how this operates. For those from the UK, please review the website and identify the functions it supports (www.dfes.benchmarking).

The benchmarking website offers school leaders the opportunity to compare their budget with schools or trusts in similar circumstances to see if spending could be more efficient.

It is possible to:

- Identify schools or trusts that are similar or with similar challenges.
- Compare your school's or trust's spending with similar schools or trusts.
- Compare the staffing structures of your school or schools within your trust with similar schools.
- Find contact details for similar schools or schools within similar trusts.

The benchmarking tool is recommended as a core planning tool in school leadership activity. It highlights four main cost areas in budget planning:

- Staff.
- Premises (for example, building maintenance).
- Occupation (the cost of occupying the school building, for example energy and water).
- Supplies and services (for example stationery, books and examination fees).

Benchmarking can be a valuable process as it enables comparisons of income and expenditure with other schools. Once furnished with comparators school leaders can consider how their resources can be used efficiently whilst also possibly identifying areas of improvement where required.

Benchmarking is a requirement in the UK for the schools financial value standard (SFVS) and should be completed by school governors before the end of the financial year. For academy schools, MATs or free schools (see Chapter 5), the new School Resource Management Self-Assessment Tool (SRMSA) should be used. Benchmarking allows leaders to understand the financial position of their school, and to identify areas of strengths and areas to improve.

The tool is offered as a guide and leaders are instructed, when using the tool, to be aware of any special circumstances that might explain why their school might appear in the upper or lower quartile for financial stability.

To carry out a benchmarking exercise the DfE advises that leaders compare their data with schools with similar characteristics such as area, school size and percentage of pupil premium children.

When evaluating the benchmarking results leaders are advised to ask the following questions:

- How does your spending compare with the spending of similar schools and what does that tell you?
- How do these results compare with the results you received last year? Are there any large changes?
- Does your spending relate to the school improvement priorities?

The benchmarking tool is intended to support future planning with the following questions offered by the DfE to support financial processes:

- How do you monitor your spending on a regular basis to ensure your finances are being used according to school priorities and stay within the specific budget set?
- How will this benchmarking data help to inform future decision-making?
- How will you make these changes to make sure your resources are used to support high-quality teaching and the best outcomes for your pupils? (www.dfe. benchmarking)

The SVFS form, completed by school governors, the head being a member of this body, possess the following questions for annual consideration:

1. Do you benchmark the size of your senior leadership team annually against that of similar schools?
2. Do you benchmark your income and expenditure annually against that of similar schools and investigate further where any category appears to be out of line?

(www.dfe.svfs.gov.uk)

Table 13.1 shows how schools can be benchmarked against one another. Multiple layers of information lie below this chart to allow leaders to compare and review their expenditure.

The school in red here represents the search school when using the tool with other schools of similar size and location mapped here based on the search criteria of 'similar funding available in the area'.

Using resources available from the DfE, school leadership teams can also access information which tells them how efficiently they are operating based on the use of resources to improve pupil progress. Staff salaries make up the largest expenditure in any school and these data can be used to plan for the recruitment of staff and

Table 13.1 Benchmarking in action

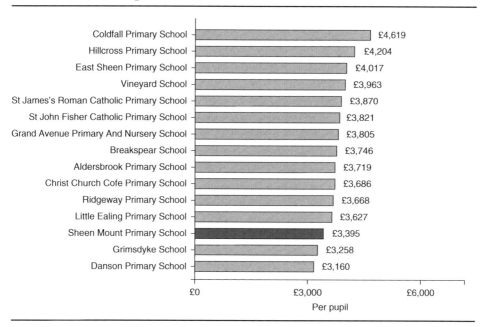

Source: DfE benchmarking tool.

the financial management of staffing structures. The tool, known as the Integrated Curriculum and Financial Planning tool (ICFP), also includes a curriculum planning tool which links the design and offer of the curriculum to workload planning giving easy access to:

1. Staff pay as a percentage of total expenditure.
2. Average teacher costs.
3. Pupil-to-teacher ratio (PTR).
4. Class size.
5. Teacher contact ratio.
6. Proportion of budget spent on the leadership team.
7. 3–5-year budget projections.
8. Spend per pupil for non-pay expenditure lines compared to similar schools.
9. School improvement plan priorities and the relative cost of options.

(www.icfp.dfe.gov.uk)

Table 13.2 compares two schools offering information on salary costs against the funding received annually to operate the school.

> **Task 13.2 Review the data**
>
> Review the foregoing data and consider what sort of questions a leadership team might wish to explore when comparing the two schools. It may be that one school has a high number of pupils with special needs and this would account for the large staff numbers. Are there other issues to consider?

Table 13.3 illustrates the pupil-to-teacher ratio (PTR) for four different schools.

Table 13.2 Expenditure in two schools

Description	School 1	School 2
Number of staff	28	50
Average gross salary	£25,000	£27,500
National Insurance and pension burden (assumed at 20%)	£5,000	£5,500
Total staff costs	£840,000	£1,650,000
Yearly budget	£1,100,000	£2,062,500
Staff costs as % of	76%	80%

Table 13.3 Pupil-to-teacher ratio comparisons

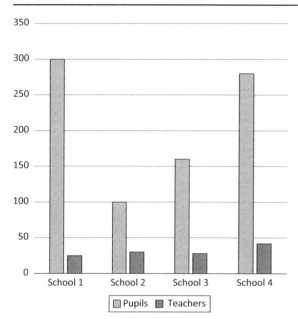

Given the foregoing data a number of questions need to be asked by the leadership teams for the respective schools. For example:

* Why are the PTRs so different in the four schools?
* What is the PTR for different key stages within each school?
* How does the school's PTR compare with similar schools? If it's significantly different, what is the reason for this?

Further relevant questions might be:

1. What is staff pay as a percentage of total expenditure?
2. What proportion of budget is spent on leadership salaries?
3. What are the expected teacher contact hours?
4. What is the PTR?
5. Class sizes across all year groups and in all subjects?

These were the questions posed by a new headteacher in the following case study.

Case study 13.1 Fitzharrys School – staffing issues

When a 'local lad' took over a school with a satisfactory OfSTED grading he reportedly knew what he was taking on. 'We were self-evaluating as a grade 4 when I took over and within a month, we realised that we were heading for a deficit budget'. All staff had to be sent redundancy letters and we started a process whereby everyone had to apply for new roles as we restructured the school to ensure we could return a balanced budget'. I started at Christmas and by the following September we had reduced the senior management team from seven to four and completely reorganised the school.

The leadership style required to act on financial matters reflects the complexities both of the era and the act of leading. Peters (2002), when writing about large organisations, determined that frictions between teams is disappearing. In applying this thesis to schools we can see what Peters described as 'the top' – this we propose might relate to leaders of large academy chains (see Chapter 5) who might not even be in the UK, who are visionary and distant. The 'old middle', according to Peters, who 'knew everything and checked everything', the traditionalists, are disappearing and being replaced by a 'new middle' who are innovators, leaders with intellectual capital and technological knowhow and also by 'the bottom', who are supported by information and knowledge and are becoming more influential. And, finally, the 'outside influencers' – government, OfSTED, academy leaders, governors, parents and even pupils – have more power. This model makes it essential that leaders act on knowledge and are able to provide evidence to support any actions they might be required to take that might impact staff workloads, staffing complement and financial management (Peters, 2018). The approach required when addressing financial matters and associated 'tough' decisions requires leadership with integrity. This might be identified as being within the scope of what is defined as 'trait leadership', discussed later in this chapter.

There are a number of actions that school leaders may have to take if operating with a deficit budget, such as:

- Closing less popular subjects.
- Increasing class sizes for certain year or subject groups.
- Teaching some year groups together in certain subjects.
- discontinuing some classes that are heavy users of school resources (arts perhaps as an examination subject).
- Reducing the number of senior leaders in the school.

This may then provide opportunities to:

* Increasing the number of maths and English periods.
* Tailoring the curriculum to give pupils extra support in subjects where they are weak in specificed subject areas, at A level

If these actions have produced savings then the leadership team may consider recruiting teachers with specific skills aimed at supporting students who need extra support, but only granting them on a one-year contract whilst requiring all members of the leadership team to teach some classes.

There are a number of case studies of leaders operating effectively to create budget-efficient schools at www.dfe.gov.uk.financialmanagement. The following case study is adapted from this website.

Case study 13.2 The Weald School

The Weald School is a large secondary school in West Sussex. The head-teacher, Peter Woodman, takes a data-informed and curriculum-led approach to staff planning.

Mr Woodman plans his staffing structure one year ahead, based on the view of his senior leadership team (SLT) whilst mindful of the ideal curriculum model for the school. The SLT considers detailed pupil attainment data, for all schools available from the government.

The SLT uses a customised spreadsheet which shows, by year group, the number of subject periods needed and the number of periods for which there are teachers available. Mr Woodman aims for an average contact ratio of 0.8, which he can adjust on the spreadsheet. He can also adjust factors such as pupil numbers and class sizes to ascertain the net level of overstaffing or understaffing by subject. This gives a picture of the school's staffing needs for the following year.

Mr Woodman and his team then examine the school's five-year budget and benchmarking data. These data include teacher contact time, class sizes and staff costs.

This approach allows Mr Woodman to know the school's staffing levels and recruitment needs at any given point in the year. He has therefore been able to make strategic curriculum changes to help pupils. He has, for example, been able to:

* Increase the number of maths and English periods in years 7 and 8.

- Tailor the curriculum for some pupils by taking them out of lessons in which they are very strong, to give them extra lessons in subjects in which they are weaker.

Mr Woodman's strategic, curriculum-led approach ensures a consistent focus on delivering the best possible curriculum in the most efficient way possible. There is virtually no overstaffing and teachers are flexible in covering for one another when there is sickness absence. Mr Woodman plans well in advance, uses data effectively and consults regularly with his SLT to meet the school's staffing needs. He keeps the school within budget while maintaining a focus at all times on pupil needs and outcomes (www.dfe.gov.uk).

 # Leader traits

The leadership approach described in the case study reflects the attributes of a leader prepared to 'do the right thing' (Bennis and Nanus, 1985), working to establish an efficient organisation by finding a way forward (Hodgon, 1987) focused clearly on a vision for the future (Bryman, 1986). Although these references may appear dated, they are relevant and contribute to what modern theorists might refer to as 'trait theory'.

One of the key traits required for leaders of education operating in challenging times is the ability to lead with honesty and integrity by keeping to promises made and always being able to justify decisions. Kramer and Enomoto (2014) refer to this as 'ethical leadership' implying that leaders may make mistakes but this is one area where you have to succeed. Ethical leadership is a core trait of successful leaders. Eight principles of ethical educational leadership are identified:

1. Courage – to do the right thing to create a positive educational environment with a willingness to reject policies which are ill-founded if they are against the interest of students whilst also being prepared to make harsh decisions, again, if they can be justified as being the best solution in the circumstances.
2. Educational interests before personal needs – what is best for the students, staff and local community should have priority of the self-interests of the school leader.
3. Self-control, self-discipline and integrity – all types of leadership essentially include these three traits in order to be considered ethical. Followers in the

wider community look to leaders in all capacities, and as such it's necessary for leaders to be a positive role model and force in the lives of the stakeholders. Relationships between leaders and followers should not rely too heavily on trust, but rather should be built on mutual respect and ethical actions.

4. Focus on tasks – school leaders should aim to create the conditions which allow teachers to succeed. This is complex as it requires paying attention to the needs of staff as well as students, whilst balancing the requirement to implement change and get things done.

5. Acknowledging the expertise of the team – ethical leaders recognise the pool of talent they can draw on, both staff and students. This requires action as well as words in the promotion of excellence whilst aiming to maximise the potential of others.

6. Setting expectations – this requires ethical standards from everyone, not just teachers and students but parents and other individuals associated with the school. Behavioural expectations need to be clearly articulated and demonstrated by everyone.

7. Awareness of the political, social and economic environment whilst demonstrating empathy and support for others – it is essential to practice equity in the treatment of other members of the school community.

8. Inclusiveness – a sense of belonging is key to gaining trust within an organisation, and trust is a driving factor in success in any context. Consideration of and respect for members of the organisation has been shown to motivate followers and lift morale, thereby increasing school performance and effectiveness.

(Adapted from the work of Kramer and Enomoto, 2014:25)

The competencies from the National Professional Qualifications for Leadership addressed in this chapter are:

> Deploy staff, financial and educational resources within a team efficiently, to enhance pupil progress.
>
> Demonstrate the ability to use resource and project management tools and techniques including budget forecasting and project plans.

Although placed near the end of this text, this chapter is central to the leadership challenges faced by leaders in our schools today. With financial pressures dominating the world agenda following periods of great uncertainty and instability, it is essential that education is funded appropriately and that the funding available is well-spent.

 References

Bennis, W. and Nanus, B. (1985) *Leaders*. New York: Harper and Row.

Bryman, A. (1986) *Leadership and organisation*. London: Routledge/Kegan Paul.

Hodgon, P. (1987) *Managers can be taught but leaders have to learn*. San Francisco, CA: Jossey-Bass.

https://libquotes.com/boutros-boutros-ghali (accessed 25th May, 2020).

https://www.un.org/sustainabledevelopment/sustainable-development-goals (accessed 25th May, 2020).

https://www.un.org/en/universal-declaration-human-rights: Universal Declaration of Human Rights | United Nations (accessed 20th May, 2020).

https://www.who.int/countries/gbr (accessed 20th May, 2020).

Kramer, B. and Enomoto, E. (2014) *Leading ethically in schools and other organizations: inquiry, case studies, and decision-making*. 2nd ed. Berlin: Rowman & Littlefield Publishing Group.

Mazzucato, M. (2018) *The value of everything*. San Francisco, CA: Jossey-Bass.

Peters, T. (2002) *Thriving on chaos: handbook for a management revolution*. San Francisco, CA: Jossey-Bass.

Peters, T. (2018) *The excellence dividend: meeting the tech tide with work that wows and jobs that last*. San Francisco, CA: Jossey-Bass.

Udogu, E.I. (2007) Presidential address which was presented at the keynote banquet held at the twenty-fifth annual meeting of ATWS in Lima, Peru. November 18–20, 2007. *Journal of Third World Studies*, 15 (1), 345–361.

Wright-Gustafsson, E. (2019) *Report to the Office for Economic Cooperation and Development*. Global Economy Development Centre for Universal Education. Belgium: OECD Publications.

www.dfe.benchmarking.gov.uk (accessed 25th May, 2020).

www.dfe.svfs.gov.uk (accessed 25th May, 2020).

www.financialplanning.dfe.gov.uk (accessed 25th May, 2020).

www.icfp.dfe.gov.uk (accessed 25th May, 2020).

United Nations Assembly. (1995) Report on fourth world conference on women, Beijing 1995. United Nations. 31 December 2003. Retrieved 27 August, 2020.

14 | **The final word**

In drawing this text to a close, a final comment on the issues facing leaders today is required. We live in challenging times, when the world might be described as being off its axis, where we cannot predict the next challenge or prepare for the next change. There will be more and different challenges ahead and we have to have hope for a future when humanity collectively reaffirms the things in life that matter, where we can trust our politicians and strive to secure a safe existence for our children, living in harmony and working for the good of all, not just for the few. In this context effective school leadership is more important than ever before.

School leaders will need to be responsive to change and motivated to develop a culture of innovation. Developing leadership behaviours that are active, confident and responsible will enhance leadership capability. School leaders will have to promote and support change and be open to new ideas which offer different perspectives.

Living in a world identified as modelling the characteristics of volatility, uncertainty, complexity and ambiguity (VUCA), with major disasters and crises occurring on a frequent basis, leaders of our schools will have to navigate an uncertain future. The reality of what a school is for and how it is organised may change. Teachers will have to cater for a wider range of student needs with certain instability impacting on the mental health of our students. Learners will respond differently to the challenges we face. Young people will have to be resilient to operate in challenging and unpredictable circumstances. For leaders, this will require personal resilience, optimism in the face of hardship and the need to be innovative in the face of change. Headteachers will have to create schools that offer a place of stability, security and calm. Establishing a school culture (see Chapter 3) with a vision, mission and ethos that seeks to stabilise the world, offer sustainable security and give children pride in their schooling will be essential.

And what of educational leadership theory? Engaging with theory is a justifiable intellectual pursuit that can offer teachers and headteachers support when facing a challenge. Theory is integral to practice and vice versa and therefore difficult to separate. The theories that grow in prevalence and gain acceptance might range from grand ideas, mid-range approaches and those close to practice. Here the focus has been on theory that aligns closely with everyday challenges faced by leaders in a rapidly changing world. The aim of theory in this context is to enable critical thinking, to generate agency and the possibility for action.

In the past theory has been somewhat secondary to the repertoire of the busy leader. It has been reduced in many cases to 'particular decisions that can be made and implemented on Monday morning' (Gunter, 2010:520). This is not what atomic leadership means; it requires planning and thought. Small steps to change may well be the most effective way forward. In the UK context large-scale reform has dominated the education agenda with changes impacting on the structural formation of schools. Schools have experienced increased testing of learners, the move to Academisation, reform of the national curriculum, teacher performance reviews, encouragement to a systems approach, quality audits, published league tables, community engagement and requirements for safeguarding alongside greater leadership accountability. It is time now to look at practice, to take an 'issues' approach to describe the lived experience of educationalists and offer advice, informed by recognised theory, to support leaders, mid-leaders and aspiring leaders in their role.

School leadership has always been dynamic, but never more so than today. With systems approaches in place (see Chapter 4) leaders can cooperate to trial new ways of learning and disseminate their successes and failures in what will have to be a new honesty and openness about what works in our schools.

School leaders will need to build innovative school cultures that don't rely on past experiences or known practices. A mindset which sees uncertainty as an advantage will be required. Collaborative dialogue to share ideas will be essential; this is how innovation will materialise and be shared. Leaders will need to be responsive to change and motivated to develop a culture of innovation. Developing leadership behaviours that are active, confident and responsive will enhance leadership capability. The promotion of new ideas and different ways of thinking, from a range of perspectives, will have to become part of the leader's detailed range of skills.

The style of dialogue required will focus on asking questions and exercising critical thinking without always expecting immediate answers. A supportive school leadership team led by a headteacher who can inspire their staff will need to create an atmosphere where questioning is encouraged, where all staff can ask 'what if?' and be part of the exploration of multiple possibilities.

The demands of the VUCA world we inhabit will require school leaders and teachers to collaborate and doubt their teaching and learning practices (Schechter and Ganon-Shilon, 2015), to trial small atomic steps and then be prepared to observe critically the positive and negative impacts.

Working in partnership headteachers will have to think about new routines, whilst challenging their habitual perceptions and assumptions to improve school effectiveness.

As well as suggesting small steps, atomic leadership offers the dimension of atomic questioning, where short, sharp and focused questions are posed. School leaders and educators will need to examine their knowledge and beliefs while leading school change. Creating a questioning culture can foster the development of a framework to allow leaders to leverage change and navigate complexity and uncertainty. Using an atomic leadership approach, school leaders might focus attention on small initiatives that have the potential to create change.

Transformational leadership will be required as a commitment from headteachers to lead their staff with enthusiasm, offering emotional support as they tackle challenges not conceived of before. Creating a safe environment for questions, for challenge, for right and wrong answers will not be easy. It will be time-consuming and demanding, requiring commitment from leaders to give new energies to test out ideas and different ways of working. Both right and wrong answers will materialise and need to be tested, whilst not stifling any enthusiasm for innovation.

In Chapter 5 a list of policy changes that impacted on a group of schools partaking in the Oxford research project was provided. These schools were defined as 'underperforming' and multiple initiatives were directed their way. It is perhaps time to ask government to stop interfering in our schools, to stop introducing new initiatives, driving always the mantra of school performance tables and pupil achievement. It is time now to trust professional educators, to limit external interference and give leaders the time and space to dedicate their energy to the challenges they face. Leaders and teachers need space and time to work collaboratively, to develop innovative approaches and to figuratively wrap their arms around the young people of today growing up in unprecedent times. It is time for the world to slow down, to reflect, to give school leaders space and confidence to collaborate as professional educators and find their own solutions in these difficult times.

As a final section to this book, some questions are posed for consideration:

Task 14.1 Time for personal reflection

Complete the following:

Leadership is nothing without…
Leaders need the following qualities…
The challenges for leaders in VUCA times are…
The role of leadership theory is to…
The issues that will demand attention in the future will be…
Successful leaders in the future will…

The core messages to take from this text

We are living through a period of unprecedented change, a VUCA environment where we can be sure of nothing and certain only of challenge and disruption to the tradition order of things. For leaders of education this means that there will be challenges not faced before. No one day will be the same, and every challenge will be one you have not met before, whether that be a financial one, a health matter, a staffing concern or one created by government initiatives or external conflicts. What this book has tried to do is offer some insights and to share good practice whilst also referencing the traditional theories of leadership so that readers might take small steps towards change. One learning point to emphasise is that success doesn't require major action. Small steps, over time, can have massive impact.

The focus here has predominately been on the UK education system. This is a system subject to immense change but still one admired by countries across the world. Leaders of education in this system have adapted to changing curricula, increased audit, financial constraints, new organisational arrangements and a unique funding approach which is gradually removing the responsibility for schooling away from regional and national politics to private organisations and charities. Quietly and somewhat unnoticed the whole nature of schooling is changing.

Across the globe new technologies are impacting also on the way leaders lead, on pedagogy and on the priorities of our learners. The dominance of the virtual is affecting the way we communicate and the way we teach. The challenge for leaders is to move with the rapid speed of change and to maintain influence where traditional processes and controls are removed. It may become expedient for school leaders to employ virtual teachers who offer training in subjects where there are teacher shortages, in teaching advanced-level mathematics for example. The leadership of learning may be transformed into the leadership of a virtually delivered curriculum, offered by experts from across the world. Such innovation will reduce the influence of school leaders and potentially diminish their role.

In this text lessons have been learned from across the globe and an international perspective offered. Partnership approaches to learning, systems leadership and practices around LGBTQ+ have been shared as ideas to model. Attempts have been made at offering solutions to some of the challenges faced by the issues that threaten our world order. Being a leader is a challenging role, no less so today than it was in the past. School leadership is an honourable role and one to aspire too, but also possibly an uncomfortable position when set against the many uncertainties. As one headteacher stated, 'I could never have been truly prepared for headship – I never know what is going to happen from one day to the next'. Given this scenario, a new approach to leadership is proposed, namely atomic leadership, which takes small bite-size steps to achieve large outcomes and create the momentum for positive change. This book is intended to offer ideas, innovations, theories and approaches which may, when tested, impact at a large scale on the challenges of leadership today.

It is not good to end a book on a dark note, but when thinking about a future for educational leadership the words of WB Yeats come to mind. In his poem 'The Second Coming', written in 1919, just after the end of the First World War and the pandemic of 1918, he wrote: 'the best lack all conviction while the worst are full of passionate intensity'.

The poem presents a vision of chaos with conventional beliefs challenged and the accepted secure way of things under attack. Imagery shows a world out of control that is disturbing, with innocence lost and the darkest of intentions prevailing. Yeats condemns the 'best' for allowing the 'worst' to press, with great intensity, for the dominance of evil.

The poem, if applied to current times, reminds us to take action. It is time to demand a new charter for education, where integrity of spirit and action reaffirms the right of young children to a safe future with all having an equal chance to make something of their lives. The future is a reality in emergence for which we all have a responsibility. As educationalists we need to place ourselves in a position of significance to be able to shape the values that will inform our world. And we need to create a future forged on things that matter – to privilege the common good, envision a future that is culturally enriching, create a clear moral ought.

It is time to reclaim the endeavour that is education, to reduce the time our children spend on things that have no real value (including the ever-increasing demands of testing) and create a pedagogy of hope – where else would we do this if not in our schools? In the words of Philip Pullman, the children's author, we must end

> the present dreary culture of mechanistic tests and meaningful league tables [...] they should be swept away like filthy cobwebs; children need light and drama and music and poetry and art and curiosity and libraries and plenty of grass to play on and time to fool around.
>
> (Pulman, 2020)

And, as a personal conclusion from the author, whatever role you inhabit in the rich and diverse world that is education, I wish you courage to maintain the path you have set for yourself and the strength to meet the challenges ahead.

References

Gunter, H. (2010) A sociological approach to educational leadership. *British Journal of Sociology of Education*, 31 (4), 519–527.

Pulman, P. (2020) *Facebook page reflections on the impact of the Coronavirus epidemic*. Open access materials. *Beijing Journal of Sustainability*, 5 (1), 79–88.

Schechter, C. and Ganon-Shilon, S. (2015) Reforming schools: the collective doubting perspective. *International Journal of Educational Management*, 29 (1), 62–72.

Index

Printed in Great Britain
by Amazon

56824897R00120